René Gaudez

A tour of
Normandy

Photographs by:

Hervé Champollion

Hervé Champollion
is represented by
TOP-RAPHO, Paris

Translated by Angela Moyon

ÉDITIONS OUEST-FRANCE
13, rue du Breil, Rennes

Table of contents

A province of many faces

A tour of Normandy? A good idea, but which of the many routes should we take? Geography and history have been particularly kind to this province. Diversity is its main feature, and the one that gives it its special charm and never-ending fascination.

Its 30,000 square kilometres (11,583 square miles) do not form a natural region like Brittany or Savoy. They stretch westwards into the Armorican Uplands and eastwards into the Paris Basin and are subdivided into a number of famous or lesser-known "areas" called "*Pays*". The Auge and Caux areas, for example, are easy to locate on a map; the Hiémois and Roumois areas pose more problems.

Cider apples.
There's a saying that "In Normandy, you need rods to harvest the apples".

A Norman farmhouse in Imbleville.

A province of many faces

The cliffs and beach at Etretat.

Normandy cannot be summed up in a single image. Crops, architectural styles, building materials, and coastal features all vary from one area to another. Orne, Eure, and Seine-Maritime all include vast stretches of forest, yet Manche is the least-wooded *département* in France. Seine-Maritime has a population density of 195 people per square kilometre; it is four times less in Orne. This is indeed a province full of contrasts.

Its coastline, from the Bresle Estuary to the Couesnon, forms a veritable border. Other boundaries are marked out, for convenience' sake, by the rivers Couesnon, Sarthe, Huisne, Avre, Seine, Epte and Bresle separating Normandy from Brittany, Maine, the Paris Basin, and Picardy. From one bank to the other, there is often very little difference in the landscape. Is the climate, then, the only feature that gives this province its unity? It is described as "maritime" and "mild" yet Normandy also has its "Siberian wastes" and its "lashing rain".

The trouble is that Normandy was totally manmade. It came into

The lake at La Herse in the Bellême Forest in Orne.

5

A tour of Normandy

The remains of the fortress in Arques-la-Bataille.

Jumièges.

being in 911 A.D. as a result of the Treaty of Saint-Clair-sur-Epte. Its territory was ceded by Charles the Simple, King of France, to Rollo, Chief of the Vikings, who already occupied part of it anyway. It was later extended by his descendants, William Longsword and William the Conqueror. Over the past ten centuries, only the Channel Islands have escaped, having been granted to King John of England by Philip Augustus in 1204 after the French sovereign had taken possession of the remainder of the duchy.

Downgraded to a mere province in 1469 by Louis XI, the territory is now subdivided into the regions of Upper and Lower Normandy for administrative reasons. Upper Normandy, which includes the *départements* of Eure and Seine-Maritime and has Rouen as its main town, covers an area of 12,258 square kilometres (4,733 square miles) for a population of 1,739,000. Lower Normandy consists of Calvados, Manche and Orne and has Caen as its main town. It covers 17,583 square kilometres (6,789 square miles) and has a population of 1,390,000.

Marked by the conquest of England, Southern Italy and Sicily, the duchy's history has left a profound mark on Normandy but this is not sufficient to define its many facets. Passage graves, menhirs and other

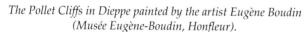

The Pollet Cliffs in Dieppe painted by the artist Eugène Boudin
(Musée Eugène-Boudin, Honfleur).

standing stones bear witness to human settlements in this area in prehistoric times. The Unelli of Viridorix fought Caesar's lieutenants as pitilessly as the Veneti struggled against the emperor himself. Lillebonne, Evreux, and Coutances were all major Gallo-Roman settlements. The monasteries in Fontenelle, Jumièges, and Fécamp were founded before the Norsemen arrived; the fearsome Vikings caused the downfall of all three.

Many of the pages in the history book of France were written in Normandy. It is true that, with the exception of Mont Saint-Michel, the area was under English control for one hundred years until Joan of Arc was burnt at the stake in Rouen on 30th May 1431, a date that marked both the peak and the turning point of the period of foreign rule. The first voyages of discovery to West Africa, the Cape of Good Hope, Brazil, the St Lawrence Seaway, and Florida were all undertaken by Norman seafarers or by navigators who set off from Normandy's ports. It was in Arques, Ivry and Louviers that Henri IV settled the crown of France firmly on his own head. It was in Brécourt near Vernon, in 1793, that the Federalist army dispersed after the battle that was never fought, the "Battle Without Tears", having failed in its attempt to defeat the supporters of the National Convention. In the same year, in Granville, soldiers and ordinary men and women repulsed an attack by royalist rebels and sent them scurrying back towards the Loire. The population suffered badly during the Prussian occupation and local resistance was described in a book by Maupassant. Finally, on 6th June

1944, it was on Norman soil that the final battle began to free the world of Nazi domination. The province paid a heavy price for this victory. A total of 35,000 civilians were killed, more than four hundred towns and villages were among the most badly-damaged in France and some, like Caen, Rouen, Saint-Lô and Le Havre, were almost entirely flattened.

In architecture, painting, literature, science, and economics, Normandy has had a role to play. This is a region steeped in mysticism with many churches and chapels dedicated to the Virgin Mary whose feast day was known as the "Normans' Feast Day". Other sanctuaries are dedicated to St Michael. Normandy is also a region that offers a certain lifestyle. There are as many castles and manor houses as there are churches and abbeys. Architects, sculptors, painters, and gardeners used as much talent in the building and embellishing of these vernacular constructions as they did in the service of God.

Tables in Normandy are weighed down with local produce including cream, butter, and cheese. Caen has made tripe famous. Rouen is known for its duckling. Dieppe is the home of sole and Mortagne of black pudding. Vire is the place for chitterlings. As to the cellars filled with kegs of cider, Calvados and *pommeau* (a mixture of apple brandy and apple juice), they are steeped in the sweet smell of the local fruit.

Mont Saint-Michel, Caen, the Landing Beaches, Lisieux, Honfleur, Rouen, Giverny, and Etretat are just a few of the essential stops on a sightseeing tour for people in a hurry. They, though, will take home an incomplete picture of Normandy for the region takes much more time to visit. Sometimes it seems as if nobody can ever really get to know it but that does not stop people from travelling up and down its highways and byways. Readers of this book will have to forgive their guide in this respect. He will have to omit so much and skim so quickly over all that the region has to offer.

Pegasus Bridge in Bénouville, the site of a British victory on the night of 6th June 1944.

Manche, the "Finistère of Normandy"

Barbey d' Aurevilly:
his works have strong links with the
département of Manche.

The *département* of Manche stretches from the borders of Brittany to the tip of the Cherbourg Peninsula, a distance south to north of 140 kilometres (87 miles). Coutances, Cherbourg and Avranches share religious, judicial and consular authority. Saint-Lô lies in the heart of the "Finistère of Normandy" and it is this central geographical situation which has made it the administrative and political centre of such a scattered *département*.

Its 330 kilometres (205 miles) of coastline have given Manche (the French name for the English Channel that laps its shores) an undoubtedly maritime vocation; the 400,000 hectares of pasture and 60,000 hectares of marshland have made it equally famous as an agricultural area. With the exception of food-processing and nuclear power, there is very little industry here. Manche claims, in fact, to be the "most ecological *département* in France".

Manche is very much part of Normandy. It was the birthplace of Tocqueville, Barbey d'Aurevilly, and Millet and, for many years, it was a fortress in the path of the "English". Over the past one hundred years, this role of stronghold has no longer had any meaning. The region has also lost many of its local people because of the distance from major towns, the decreasing numbers of jobs in farming, and the depletion of the fishing fleets. It now has a population of 480,000; a century ago, its population numbered 600,000.

For visitors, it contains some of the finest sights in Normandy and Mont Saint-Michel is a right royal introduction to Manche.

Manche, the "Finistère of Normandy"

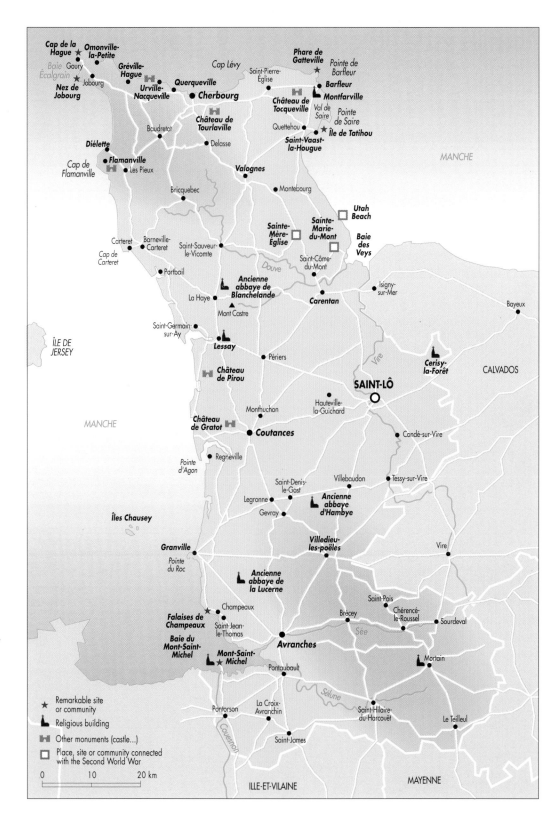

Cap de la Hague
Omonville-la-Petite
Baie d'Écalgrain
Goury
Gréville-Hague
Jobourg
Nez de Jobourg
Urville-Nacqueville
Querqueville
Cherbourg
Cap Lévy
Saint-Pierre-Église
Phare de Gatteville
Pointe de Barfleur
Barfleur
Montfarville
Château de Tocqueville
Val de Saire
Pointe de Saire
Quettehou
Île de Tatihou
Saint-Vaast-la-Hougue
Château de Tourlaville
Baudretot
Delasse
Diélette
Flamanville
Les Pieux
Cap de Flamanville
Valognes
Bricquebec
Montebourg
Carteret
Barneville-Carteret
Saint-Sauveur-le-Vicomte
Cap de Carteret
Portbail
Sainte-Mère-Église
Sainte-Marie-du-Mont
Utah Beach
Baie des Veys
Saint-Côme-du-Mont
Douve
Isigny-sur-Mer
Bayeux
Ancienne abbaye de Blanchelande
La Haye
Mont Castre
Carentan
MANCHE
ÎLE DE JERSEY
Saint-Germain-sur-Ay
Lessay
Périers
Vire
Cerisy-la-Forêt
CALVADOS
Château de Pirou
SAINT-LÔ
Hauteville-la-Guichard
Monthuchon
Château de Gratot
Coutances
Condé-sur-Vire
MANCHE
Regnéville
Pointe d'Agon
Saint-Denis-le-Gast
Villebaudon
Tessy-sur-Vire
Legronne
Gevray
Ancienne abbaye d'Hambye
Îles Chausey
Granville
Villedieu-les-poëles
Vire
Pointe du Roc
Ancienne abbaye de la Lucerne
Saint-Pois
Chérencé-le-Roussel
Champeaux
Brécey
Sourdeval
Falaises de Champeaux
Saint-Jean-le-Thomas
Sée
Baie du Mont-Saint-Michel
Avranches
Mont-Saint-Michel
Pontaubault
Mortain
Pontorson
La Croix-Avranchin
Sélune
Saint-Hilaire-du-Harcouët
Le Teilleul
Couesnon
Saint-James
ILLE-ET-VILAINE
MAYENNE

★ Remarkable site or community
⛪ Religious building
🏰 Other monuments (castle...)
□ Place, site or community connected with the Second World War

0   10   20 km

A tour of Normandy

MONT-SAINT-MICHEL

This pyramid set in the sand or jutting up from the waves, depending on the tide, is easily identifiable at a single glance. The western world has, indeed, made this its emblem. How many billions of feet have trodden its streets before you added your steps to the number? Only in the winter months does the Mont regain a semblance of solitude. It has been a place of worship and refuge for more than 2,000 years and has had a church dedicated to St Michael for 1,300 of them. It has also been a fortress and a prison. It is an architectural masterpiece that attracts two million visitors every year. Christian believers still come here to pray to the archangel or celebrate liturgical feast days with the community of Benedictines who returned to the island in 1966.

From shore to archangel: 152 metres - 494 ft. and 1,000 years of work.

The Marvel.

The marvel of the Marvel: the cloisters.

Its origins are shrouded in legend. It is said that a tidal wave swallowed up the Scissy Forest in 709 A.D. and turned the rocky outcrop of Mount Tombe into an island. It was here, one year earlier, that Bishop Aubert of Avranches had erected a sanctuary in honour of St. Michael. The illustrious celestial being had been most insistent that the prelate should comply with his wishes - he had stuck his finger into the bishop's skull to press home his point.

In the 11th Century, the Mont became a permanent building site stacked with soft Caen stone and hard Chausey granite. Buildings

Joint service in the minster.

were constructed to provide good-quality accommodation for the increasing numbers of pilgrims who came here and the abbey set up a network of buildings as labyrinthine as the chapters of its history book. Most of the work was undertaken by the Benedictines who were installed here by Richard II in 966 A.D.

The Main Steps and the steeper flight of 90 steps beyond them lead to the holy of holies, the abbey church, set 330 feet above sea level. The church is a feat of technical prowess on which work began in 1017 and was completed a century later.

Building work began on the Marvel in 1211, thanks to a donation from Philip Augustus. It took less than twenty years to complete and contains the famous cloisters, refectory, Guests' Room, and Knights' Room, an admirable example of Gothic architecture. By that time, Mont Saint-Michel had (almost) acquired its final outline. The spire above the minster, on

"(...) A fantastic pyramid topped by a cathedral" (Guy de Maupassant, Notre coeur).

which the statue of the Archangel rises to a height of 157 metres (510 ft.) above the shore, was not added until 1897.

During the One Hundred Years' War, the Mont became a fortress, with army chiefs being quickly sent to support the abbot who had become the head of a garrison. They included Du Guesclin (his wife's house (Maison de Tiphaine) is open to the public), Nicolas Paynel and, more particularly, Louis d'Estoute-ville who, assisted by one hundred and nineteen Norman knights, withstood a twenty-year siege laid by the English from the neighbouring islet of Tombelaine. The gatehouse, towers above the gateway to the minster and most of the outer walls date from this period.

Once the One Hundred Years' War and Wars of Religion were over, the abbey lost its splendour and never regained it. It was abandoned by the monks and turned into a prison by Napoleon. Louis XI had already had a few of his infamous iron cages installed here. It was not until 1874 that Mont Saint-Michel was listed as a "historic monument" and saved from ultimate ruin. It took one hundred years to complete the restoration work.

At low tide, visitors strain their eyes to catch a glimpse of the sea which, these days, only lashes the walls at very high tides. The 40,000 hectares of bay are silting up. Will Mont Saint-Michel stand one day in the middle of pastures amid flocks of salt meadow sheep? Work is currently underway to ensure that the "Marvel of the Western World" remains "St. Michael in peril of the sea".

The spire and Frémiet's statue of St. Michael, the Archangel which was restored in 1987.

The tiny island of Tombelaine and Mont Saint-Michel Bay, once covered by the legendary Scissy Forest.

A manuscript from Mont Saint-Michel Abbey, now kept in Avranches Library.

MONT SAINT-MICHEL VISIBLE FROM ALL DIRECTIONS

Whether you are in Avranches or Mortain, or on the Isles Chausey etc., Mont Saint-Michel juts up above the horizon unless it is shrouded in mist. One of the best views is to be had from Avranches, which is not far away and, what is more, built on a rock. Try going to the botanical gardens in the moonlight. Maupassant has been there before you and has described the view in his novel, *Notre coeur*. It is an unforgettable experience!

The town is a sub-prefecture with a population of 14,000 and has established close links with the abbey. The treasure kept in the basilica church of St. Gervais and St. Protais includes St. Aubert's skull — with the finger mark in it. The museum-cum-library has two hundred and fifty-six illuminated manuscripts and incunabulae from the monastery including the *Cartulary* and Robert of Torigni's *Chronicles*, a priceless heritage.

Between Saint-Jean-le-Thomas and Carolles, the RD 911 Granville road has been given the title of "the most attractive kilometre in France" because of the view over the abbey and bay.

Beyond Jullouville and Saint-Pair, both of which are family seaside resorts, the road leaves the coastline that it has been hugging so closely for miles and enters Granville, nicknamed the "Monaco of the North" during the 19th Century because of its resemblance to the principality. Granville was created by the English. They built a fortress in the Middle Ages, on the deserted wastes across its headland.

Beneath the rock, Granville harbour at low tide.

The stronghold was quickly captured by the French but the English also dug the "Trench", the passage which leads from the town to the Plat Gousset. The barracks high above the harbour are now used for civilian purposes but they bear witness to Granville's military history. In 1793, the town was attacked by royalist rebels who hoped to find the English fleet here, and the Emigré army. Sailors, soldiers and civilians joined forces to repulse the attack and, later, to put out the vast fire that had been lit to defend the walls round the Upper Town.

Fishing off the Grand Banks, fishing for wild oysters and privateering all brought prosperity to Granville, as is obvious in the decorative features of Notre-Dame and the superb private mansions in the Upper Town. Other reminders of this period can be seen in the Old Granville Museum. The decline in all these sectors of activity, though, led the town into decline. Fishing for shellfish (the famous clams), thalassotherapy com-bined with physiotherapy treatment and tourism now provide the community with most of its income.

Granville highlights its connections with Michelet who wrote *La Mer* here, the artist Maurice Denis who was born here by accident, and Christian Dior, the fashion designer, whose family home (Les Rhum's) is open to the public. Richard Anacréon, another of Granville's sons who became a patron of artists and writers this century, bequeathed to the town the collection that forms the basis of the exhibition in the museum named after him.

From the lighthouse, the Isles Chausey, Granville's maritime district, can be seen 18 kilometres (11 miles) out to sea. During the spring tides (the tidal range is the highest in Europe), the ebbing sea leaves some 5,000 hectares of shore and 365 reefs uncovered. Only 52 remain after the sea flows, including the only island to be inhabited, Grande Ile which is 2 kilometres (1 mile) long and 800 metres (867 yds.) wide.

The lighthouse at the top of the rock.

The Isles Chausey. (Photo Gaudez)

Manche, the "Finistère of Normandy"

VILLEDIEU, IN THE DAYS OF THE KNIGHTS OF MALTA!

If you turn your back on the sea and take the Granville-Caen or Avranches-Vire road, you will come to Villedieu-les-Poêles, a delightful example of inland towns in Manche with granite houses, picturesque courtyards, and marketday hustle and bustle.

Copperware is everywhere; it even spills out onto the pavements. Yet the production of milk churns, vases, pots and pans, or cauldrons now occupies only a very small number of companies here as a result of competition from third-world countries. The finest hours of this craft are kept alive in one work-shop, and two museums.

The ruins of Hambye Abbey.

Finishing off a bell.

Villedieu has one of the last bell foundries still in existence. Its work-shops are open to the public and visitors can enjoy the veritable cere-monial that surrounds the casting of a bell. The foundry dates back to the days of the Knights of St. John of Jerusalem, the forerunners of the Order of the Knights of Malta whose solemn procession, the Grand Sacrament, is held in Villedieu every four years.

There are two abbeys not far from the town, La Lucerne d'Outre-Mer and Hambye. A priest has given a great deal of time and effort to restoring what was left of La Lucerne after the Revolution. It was called "d'Outremer" (literally

A tour of Normandy

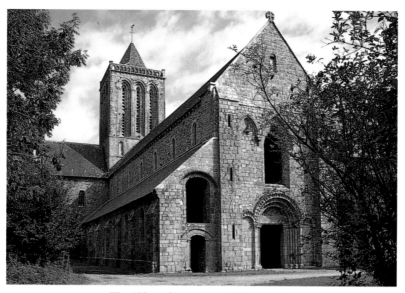

The Abbey of La Lucerne d'Outre-Mer.

"from across the sea") because of its support for the cause of the Kings of England during the One Hundred Years' War. The priest has made it a place of theological reflection and prayer, as well as an arts centre. Hambye, in the Sienne Valley, was saved from total ruin by a couple of doctors. Here again

the Revolution left little of the Benedictine monastery standing except for the square bell-tower, the Romanesque nave and the Gothic chancel in the minster. The abbey buildings house the collections belonging to the *département's* Museum of vestments and liturgical ornaments.

The R. Vire has been turned into a canal where it flows past the foot of the main town in Manche, adding a touch of prestige. After building protective walls and towers, Saint-Lô developed on a high spur of shale overlooking the river but very little remains of this first settlement, known as the "Enclosure" (L'Enclos). Because of its strategic position, Saint-Lô was extensively bombed in June and July 1944 and was eventually nicknamed the "Capital of Ruins". In order to bear witness to the tragedy and be a memorial to its victims, the collegiate church of Notre-Dame has been only partially rebuilt.

Saint-Lô was reconstructed in haste and, for many years, left visitors with an impression of gloom and austerity. The layout of a

A mosaic by Fernand Léger in the Franco-American Memorial Hospital in Saint-Lô.

The Norman Milkmaid, by Louis Derbré.

pedestrian precinct and an arts centre containing the famous tapestries called "The Love Affair of Gombault and Macée" has tempered this impression but it is forgivable to wonder whether Saint-Lô, the birthplace of astronomer Le Verrier and novelist Octave Feuillet, has really found its soul again. It has at least regained one link with its past, though, thanks to the inauguration, in 1987, of a new statue of *The Norman Milkmaid*, a woman carrying a milk churn, the symbol of a region which is overwhelmingly involved in the production and processing of milk.

The stud in this predominantly milk-producing area is one of the largest in France as regards the number of stallions kept there. It was set up by Napoleon in 1806 and is housed in superb Louis XIII buildings. Occasionally, the horses (and the collection of horse-drawn carriages) are used for pageants in town.

A carriage procession in the stud farm.

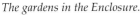
The gardens in the Enclosure.

Everyday work.

COUTANCES, THE "SUPREME EXAMPLE OF GOTHIC ARCHITECTURE"

Set at the end of a labyrinth of narrow country lanes, Hauteville-la-Guichard seems to be fleeing the glory brought to it by its famous sons. There is little left today, except a plaque in the church, to remind visitors that Guillaume, Preux, Onfroy and Robert, four of the fifteen children of Tancrède de Hauteville, created kingdoms for themselves in Apulia, Calabria and Sicily.

The lantern tower on the cathedral.

The cathedral is Coutances' pride and joy and, from the very outset, it benefited from the generosity of the local lads who had become sovereigns. Built from 1056 onwards, on the hillock on which the town had been constructed during the Gallo-Roman period, it has a tall spire 72 metres (234 ft.) high and a lantern-tower known as "The Lead". It has been described as the "supreme example of Norman Gothic architecture". After the breathtaking view from the gardens around the former bishop's palace, visitors are struck by a feeling of lightness and verticality as soon as they pass through the porch. This feeling is reinforced by the bundles of colonnettes in the nave and the tall windows in the chancel. The Gothic masterpiece, on which building work began in 1218, did not remove all the traces of the initial, Romanesque sanctuary that had been ravaged by fire. The cathedral was badly damaged in 1944 and has been restored under the watchful eye of Louis Arretche, the architect who designed the Church of Joan of Arc in Rouen.

Coutances is a lively town full of shops, and it acts rather like a draught lobby between the coast and the inland pastures. Here, as in Avranches, the botanical gardens are a "must".

Lessay, a few miles away, is set between the peaceful haven that is Saint-Germain and the moors made famous by Barbey d'Aurevilly. Here,

Gratot: the legend of the fairy.

the grave austerity of Romanesque architecture forms a contrast to the elegance of the Gothic style. Its abbey, dedicated to the Holy Trinity, is, like the abbey in Cerisy-la-Forêt near Saint-Lô, one of the finest religious buildings in this style in the whole of Normandy. Yet it was almost destroyed when, in 1944, it was blown up because it stood in the way of the artillery batteries. It took thirteen years to rebuild the monastery that had been founded by Richard de Turstin in 1056 for Benedictine monks from Bec-Hellouin Abbey.

Every year, during the second weekend in September, several hundred thousand visitors flock to Lessay for the age-old Holyrood Fair (*Foire de la Sainte-Croix*), a major event in the rural calendar.

There are two castles in the vicinity that should be included in any sightseeing tour because of their ruins and because of the legends that surround them. They are Gratot and Pirou.

Pirou: the legend of the geese.

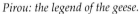

Lessay Abbey.

A tour of Normandy

IN THE FOOTSTEPS OF THE "LORD HIGH CONSTABLE OF LITERATURE"

Not far from Mount Castre where the view is panoramic and the history of particular interest, you can hear the bell in Blanchelande Abbey call the congregation to Mass as it did in the days of the abbot of La Croix-Jugan, the priest who was damned in *L'Ensorcelée*.

Barbey d'Aurevilly was born nearby, in Saint-Sauveur-le-Vicomte, on 2nd November 1808, the "Feast Day of the Dead" as he liked to point out. Set on the banks of the R. Douve, the village belonged to a whole succession of troublesome barons (the Néels, the Harcourts) whose castle, which was turned into a hospice during the reign of Louis XIV, can still be seen today (towers and keep).

During his youth, the future "Constable of Letters" divided his time between Saint-Sauveur and Valognes. He was buried in the former and it is here that you will find most of the memorabilia relating to the author. A fairly nondescript house beyond the Grande-Rue contains his manuscripts, notebooks, drawings and clothes.

Saint-Sauveur-le-Vicomte: the castle.

Mont Castre, where the Romans defeated the Unelli.

Saint-Sauveur is also the setting for a religious pilgrimage. People come here to pray to St. Marie-Madeleine Postel, founder of the Order of the Sisters of Mercy. The nun is buried in the transept of the abbey founded in the 12th Century which she restored in order to make it the mother-abbey of her Order.

Valognes, just a few miles away, fully deserved the rather derisory nickname of "the Versailles of Normandy". It was once the favourite haunt of noblemen who aped the manners and lifestyle of the Court.

Yet the title is very appropriate. The town and its church were bombed in 1944 and badly damaged. The restoration work undertaken on the church has resulted in a happy combination of ancient and modern and Valognes still has some forty private mansions built in the 17th and 18th Centuries. This is a quite outstanding architectural heritage for a town of this rather modest size. Many of the mansions can just be seen, peeping over a wall, or beneath the trees, but the Beaumont Residence is open to the public. Its frontage is 50 metres (54 yds.) long and it has a monumental staircase. Other mansions include the Maison du Grand Quartier which has been turned into the Cider Museum and the Thieuville Residence now housing the Museum of Calvados and Museum of Leather. As to the Granville-Caligny Residence, this was where Barbey stayed when he returned to Normandy.

A still and a barrel.

The Hôtel de Beaumont.

CHERBOURG, BETWEEN LA HAGUE AND THE SAIRE VALLEY

Cherbourg lies in the centre of the north coast of the peninsula of the same name, looking westwards to La Hague and eastwards to the Saire Valley, two areas that contrast sharply.

The town is one of those urban developments that people tend to judge too quickly after seeing it from a hilltop like the Montagne du Route or strolling through its centre which is devoid of architectural interest. It is also beset by "meteorological clichés" thanks to a famous film (*The Umbrellas of Cherbourg*) or the daily weather map on the television. It is the fourth largest town in Normandy as regards population (100,000) and is first and foremost a port. Vast projects designed by Vauban, launched and then abandoned by Louis XVI, restarted by Napoleon Bonaparte, and inaugurated by Napoleon III have protected it over the years from attack by ocean waves .... and the British. The Grand Dyke, which is 3,600 metres (over 2 miles) long and 27 metres (88 ft.) high with the added protection of a line of forts, is, with the Homet and Dutchmen's Dykes, the main section of the project.

By a strange twist of fate it was the Germans who, in 1944, finally used Cherbourg as the fortress town it was designed to be. Terrible fighting took place before the town could be liberated. It was quickly set back on its feet despite the considerable damage caused by the occu-

Cherbourg seen from Le Roule Fort.

It is also a fishing harbour...

pying forces and, until the Battle of the Ardennes, the harbour played a vital role in getting supplies through to the Allied armies. On the west bank of the R. Divette is the armaments depot, a reminder of Cherbourg's vocation as a naval base. The shipyard here builds missile-launching submarines, the first of which was *Le Redoutable.*

Cherbourg is a commercial port, a fishing harbour and the second largest yachting marina in France after Cannes. It is also perpetuating an old tradition by catering for the last surviving liners in its transatlantic terminal. It is, though, the ferry links to England and Ireland that provide the largest amount of traffic. On Place Napoléon, the statue shows the emperor raising his arm in the direction of "perfidious

Tourlaville Castle.

The Holy Trinity reredos.

Albion", ready to smile at the peaceful invasion of British tourists.

The remains of the Abbey of Notre-Dame-du-Voeu are, like the Church of the Holy Trinity (*église de la Trinité*) and its reredos just some of the cultural sights of Cherbourg but the most outstanding attraction is the Thomas-Henry Museum. In addition to thirty-three paintings by François Millet, the museum houses works by Fra Angelico, Murillo, Chardin, Poussin, Greuze etc. In quite a different vein, the Emmanuel Liais Park (he was a naturalist and Mayor of Cherbourg) contains some 4,600 species of plants, many of which are tropical.

Tourlaville Castle not far away is a beautiful Renaissance house

steeped in memories of Julien and Marguerite Ravalet, the grandson and grand-daughter of its founder. They were decapitated on the Place de Grève, accused of having succumbed to their mutual passion.

With the same light, the same dry stone walls, the same stumpy trees bent eastwards by the wind, and the same cliffs gashed by coves filled with the roar of the sea, La Hague is decidedly reminiscent of Brittany or Ireland. Reminiscent, that is, except for the longer grass, the larger number of livestock, and the manor houses or castles. Among them are the delightful Nacqueville and the austerely luxurious Flamanville. And from Cherbourg to Flamanville, or from the church

A tour of Normandy

The lighthouse at the Gros du Raz.

The headland known as the Nez de Jobourg.

in Querqueville to the Nez de Jobourg, panoramic views abound.

Nowhere better than in Goury can you see the fury of the sea lashing the shores of the Cherbourg Peninsula on a stormy day. Only a few yards from the harbour stands the Gros du Raz lighthouse, resisting the sheer, scurrying waves pouring along the Blanchard Race.

Diélette, further south, is as drenched by the waves as Goury. For many years, there was an underwater iron mine here; nowadays, the Flamanville nuclear power station lies on its outskirts. With Cogema's plutonium reprocessing plant near Jobourg, it makes Manche "the most nuclear *département* in France".

The artist Jean-François Millet was born in the hamlet of Gruchy near Gréville-Hague and often took La Hague as the subject of his work.

Legends are so rife in this area that there are those who have come here and have never left again because they fell totally and utterly under its spell! One such was Jacques

Prévert, the poet. Every autumn in what is said to be the Peninsula's most attractive village, Omonville-la-Petite, the falling leaves skim over his grave.

To the north-east of the peninsula is Gatteville Lighthouse, one of the tallest in France rising to a heigt of 71m. 230 ft. above the headland and race at Barfleur. It was off these cliffs that the *Blanche Nef* once sank. Further south, from the hill at La Pernelle, there is a superb panoramic view of the Saire Valley. Because it is sheltered from the prevailing winds and low temperatures, it has become a fertile fruit and vegetable-growing area.

In Barfleur, on certain particularly stormy days, the sea lashes the walls of the Church of St. Nicholas. This is a port; it is also a very attractive town with a number of beautiful houses along Cours Sainte-Catherine. In the hamlet of La Bretonne, the house where Marie-Madeleine Postel, founder of the Order of the Sisters of Mercy, was born in 1756 is now open to the public. The church in Montfarville

Repairing fishing nets.

In Sainte-Mère-Eglise,
a model serves as a reminder of the
unfortunate parachutist who dropped
onto the bell-tower and remained
hanging there for several hours.

The harbour and town of Barfleur.

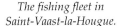

The fishing fleet in
Saint-Vaast-la-Hougue.

on the outskirts of Barfleur is surprising for its decorative features. Its walls and vaulted roof are covered with paintings by Guillaume Fouace, who was born in Réville and was one of Millet's pupils. As to Tocqueville Castle, it was the home of Alexis Carel de Tocqueville, a historian and philosopher seen by many as the father of liberalism.

Further south are the roadstead of Saint-Vaast-la-Hougue and the island of Tatihou. In 1692, the roadstead was the scene of one of the French fleet's worst disasters. Having surprised the Anglo-Dutch armada near Cherbourg, Admiral de Tourville's ships inflicted heavy losses on the enemy. However, his vessels were then forced to break off the battle and many of them were unable to cross the Blanchard Race because of the counter-current. They were pushed back by the sea and ended up in Saint-Vaast Bay where the English promptly set them alight.

Carentan is a leading food-processing centre, as well as a yachting marina.... set in the middle of the countryside. The octagonal bell-tower of its church overlooks mile upon immense mile of marshland which, in 1991, became the "Cotentin and Bessin Marshes Country Park". The best time of year to visit the marshes is in the springtime when they "blossom" and flora and fauna come back to life.

Sainte-Marie-du-Mont and Sainte-Mère-Église can be the last stops in this tour of Manche, before setting off to Calvados. In June 1944, history linked their destiny to the fate of many towns and villages in the neighbouring *département* when they became the scene of several episodes in the Allied landings. It was from the beach at La Madeleine (named "Utah Beach" for the occasion) that the Americans left to link up with the paratroopers who had been dropped during the night in and around Sainte-Mère-Église.

Calvados, great pages of histoiry...

The Normandy Bridge was opened in 1995 and links Upper and Lower Normandy (Le Havre - Honfleur) via the Seine Estuary. With a total length of 2,141 m. 2,319 yds., this is the longest cable-stayed bridge in the world and it has already become one of the most popular tourist sights in Normandy.

It was a few rocks offshore from the Bessin area that gave Calvados its name, not the famous apple-based drink of which the *département* is the major producer!

This is the smallest of all the *départements* in Normandy with an area of 5,548 square kilometres (2,142 square miles) but, like the others, it is very varied.

The 620,000 inhabitants of Calvados live in 705 towns and villages but one-third of them live in Caen and its suburbs. Caen is the "county town", the administrative capital of a Lower Normandy region which tends to focus on this one spot. Its coal or iron mines, some of which were age-old institutions, closed recently. Its steelworks shut down only yesterday, forcing the region to look for a new type of economic structure.

For sightseers, Calvados has a plethora of "trails-on-a-theme" including the Cider Trail, the Tradition Trail, the Dukes of Normandy Trail etc.

It has abbeys, churches, and castles, indeed it enjoys an unusually rich heritage. Modern history has added a few great pages to the book that began in the days of William the Conqueror. From 6th June to 21st August 1944, from the beaches of the Bessin area to the outskirts of Falaise, Calvados was, like Manche and to a lesser extent Orne, the scene of a "Battle of Normandy" that was to give the world back its freedom. This victory was to cost Calvados dear in human lives and buildings.

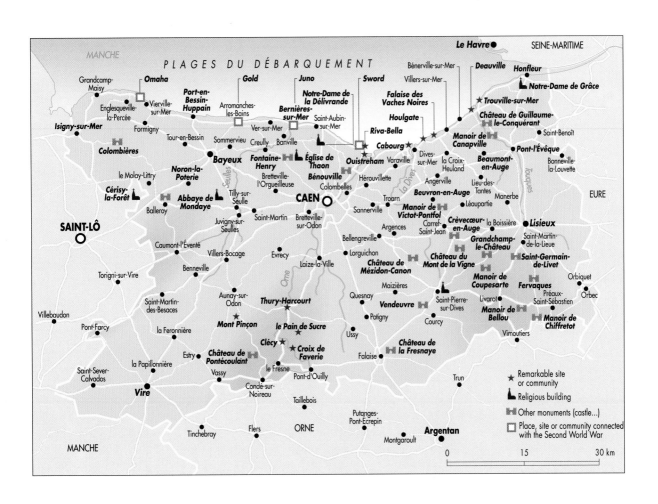

MANCHE

SEINE-MARITIME

Le Havre

PLAGES DU DÉBARQUEMENT

Bénerville-sur-Mer
Deauville
Honfleur
Notre-Dame de Grâce

Grandcamp-Maisy
Omaha
Gold
Juno
Sword
Villers-sur-Mer

Vierville-sur-Mer
Port-en-Bessin-Huppain
Arromanches-les-Bains
Notre-Dame de la Délivrande
Falaise des Vaches Noires
Trouville-sur-Mer

Englesqueville-la-Percée
Formigny
Bernières-sur-Mer
Saint-Aubin-sur-Mer
Houlgate
Château de Guillaume-le-Conquérant

Isigny-sur-Mer
Tour-en-Bessin
Ver-sur-Mer
Riva-Bella
Saint-Benoît

Colombières
Sommervieu
Creully
Banville
Cabourg
Manoir de Canapville
Pont-l'Évêque

Bayeux
Fontaine-Henry
Église de Thaon
Ouistreham
Varaville
Dives-sur-Mer
la Croix-Heuland
Beaumont-en-Auge
Bonneville-la-Louvette

le Molay-Littry
Noron-la-Poterie
Bretteville-l'Orgueilleuse
Bénouville
Hérouvillette
Angerville
Lieu-des-Tantes
Manerbe

Cérisy-la-Forêt
Abbaye de Mondaye
Tilly-sur-Seulle
Colombelles
Beuvron-en-Auge
Léaupartie
EURE

Balleroy
Saint-Martin
CAEN
Bretteville-sur-Odon
Troarn
Manoir de Victot-Pontfol
la Boissière
Lisieux

SAINT-LÔ
Juvigny-sur-Seulles
Sannerville
Crèvecœur-en-Auge
Saint-Martin-de-la-Lieue

Caumont-l'Éventé
Villers-Bocage
Bellengreville
Argences
Carref-Saint-Jean
Grandchamp-le-Château
Saint-Germain-de-Livet

Torigni-sur-Vire
Benneville
Evrecy
Laize-la-Ville
Lorguichon
Château de Mézidon-Canon
Château du Mont de la Vigne
Orbiquet

Villebaudon
Saint-Martin-des-Besaces
Maizières
Manoir de Coupesarte
Fervaques
Orbec

Pont-Farcy
Aunay-sur-Odon
Thury-Harcourt
Quesnay
Vendeuvre
Saint-Pierre-sur-Dives
Livarot
Préaux-Saint-Sébastien

la Feronnière
Mont Pinçon
le Pain de Sucre
Potigny
Courcy
Manoir de Bellou
Manoir de Chiffretot

la Papillonnière
Estry
Château de Pontécoulant
Clécy
Croix de Faverie
Ussy
Château de la Fresnaye
Vimoutiers

Saint-Sever-Calvados
Vassy
le Fresne
Falaise
Trun

Vire
Condé-sur-Noireau
Pont-d'Ouilly
Taillebois

Tinchebray
Flers
ORNE
Putanges-Pont-Ecrepin
Argentan
Montgaroult

MANCHE

★ Remarkable site or community

⬛ Religious building

🏰 Other monuments (castle...)

☐ Place, site or community connected with the Second World War

0   15   30 km

A tour of Normandy

THE MOTHER-OF-PEARL COAST AND THE LANDING BEACHES

Of the five bridgeheads in the *Overlord* operation, four were situated between the Orne and Vire estuaries — Sword, Juno and Gold where the British and Canadians landed, and Omaha Beach, soon to be known as "Bloody Omaha" because of the very heavy losses sustained by the Americans there.

The sea wiped out nearly all traces of this battle long ago. There are still a few wrecks visible at low tide but every storm does just a bit more damage to the mulberry harbours that made up the Winston Churchill artificial port built in Britain and floated across to Arromanches through a storm-racked Channel. On land, there are a few more reminders of the battle. There are concrete bunkers that were once part of the Atlantic Wall, like the one in Longues-sur-Mer, and stretches of land like Pointe du Hoc full of hillocks and craters caused by shells. The remainder, i.e. the essential features of the battle, the living hell for all those involved in it, can only be gleaned from the last survivors, the few eye witnesses, the countless books and the numerous museums in Arromanches, Port-en-Bessin, Vierville, Bénouville, Ouistreham, Bayeux, Mont-Ormel, Grandcamp-Maisy, Merville-Franceville, Saint-Martin-des-Besaces, Surrain, and Tilly-sur-Seulles or the Mémorial in Caen.

Mulberry harbours in Arromanches.

The American war graves in Saint-Laurent.

The Pointe du Hoc.

The Bessin coastline requires a twofold visit. Once peace had returned, the towns and villages between Isigny and Caen linked by the RD 514 regained their earlier lifestyles and became ports and seaside resorts again.

Over the past three centuries, Isigny has been reputed for its butter and cream.

It now attracts ornithologists who come to watch the waterfowl in Veys Bay. Port-en-Bessin (known to the locals as "Port") is filled with hustle and bustle when its fishing fleet sets sail or returns to port — this is, after all, the largest fishing harbour in Lower Normandy. Bernières is proud of its bell-tower, one of the tallest in Normandy at 67 metres (218 ft.). Courseulles has oyster beds and there is an interesting diorama on this particular shellfish in the Sea Centre (Maison de la Mer). The ferry link set up by a Breton company from Ouistreham-Riva-Bella, a seaside resort and large marina, has turned it into a busy terminal for those travelling between France and England.

St. Samson's is an old fortress-church which was altered in the 12th and 19th Centuries. It has an especially fine gabled façade and a chancel that is narrower than the nave.

On the other bank of the R. Orne is Bénouville Castle, now the property of Calvados County Council. It was designed in the 18th Century by the architect, Jean-Nicolas Ledoux.

A treat from Normandy.

Port-en-Bessin.

The Memorial to Peace in Caen.

BAYEUX - HISTORY'S FAVOURITE!

Bayeux is the main town in the Bessin area and one of the few towns at which destiny seems to have looked kindly throughout history. War spared the treasures bequeathed to it by the past and Charles de Gaulle added a few pages to a history that began in the days of the Gallic Bajocasses tribe. Bayeux is also one of the towns whose name is indissociable from a masterpiece. People speak of the "Bayeux tapestry" in the same way they talk about the Roman arena in Nîmes or the bridge in Avignon.

The word "tapestry" is actually incorrect. The work is really a piece of embroidery in wool on linen cloth. In the same way, the traditional story that Queen Matilda (the Penelope of Normandy) and her ladies-in-waiting did the embroidery themselves to retell the tale of the conquest of England by Matilda's husband, William, is nothing more than pious legend. The "Tale of the Conquest" was actually commissioned by Odo, William's half-brother and Bishop of Bayeux, to decorate the brand-new cathedral and was doubtless made by a workshop in a Saxon or Norman monastery.

The Tapestry is 70 metres (76 yds.) long and 50 centimetres (18 ins.) high. It has been beautifully restored and is displayed to its full advantage. It should be seen as a

The Bayeux Tapestry.

Bayeux Cathedral.

The Adam and Eve House.

documentary... and as a lesson in morality since its main theme is the keeping of a promise.

Little remains of the building that it was designed to decorate except for the towers on the West Front and the crypt. Like so many others, Bayeux Cathedral has undergone numerous alterations - some more successful than others. The "Bonnet" that was added to the cathedral in the 19th Century looks heavy above the 15th-century central tower with its ethereal, traceried bays. The light, airy nave was built in the 12th and 13th Centuries and its decoration makes it a fine example of Norman Romanesque sculpture. The chancel, on the other hand, is a model of Gothic architecture. As to the huge high altar, it was made by Caffieri in the 18th Century.

In Bayeux, though, the whole town is worth a visit. On Quai de l'Aure and Place des Tribunaux, there are superb stone-built houses alternating with a few half-timbered constructions. There is a covered market next to an old watermill. The Deanery houses both the Museum of Religious Art and the Bayeux Lace Museum. The Baron-Gérard Museum on

The Battle of Normandy Memorial Museum.

A tour of Normandy

Place des Tribunaux contains Bayeux porcelain and Aubusson tapestries, as well as paintings by Philippe de Champaigne, Van Dongen etc.

Le Molay-Littry a few miles from the town used to have the only coalmine in Normandy. A museum now retraces the history of the mine and the Norman pit workers.

Balleroy Castle was the first country house ever designed by François Mansart and it dates back to 1626. The austerity of the exterior forms a sharp contrast to the ornate interior. The gardens were laid out by Le Nôtre. The house acquired a new vocation in 1970 when it was purchased by the eminently rich American publisher, Malcolm Forbes, and became a meeting-place for those with a passion for a form of travel that is lighter than air. Its stables now contain a museum of hot-air and gas-powered balloons.

In Noron-la-Poterie, potters have been working at their craft since the Middle Ages, producing salt-glazed earthenware pots, jars, pitchers and other recipients with an attractive dark brown and bronze-coloured finish.

Six or seven miles to the south of Bayeux is Mondaye Abbey which has been a place of prayer for eight hundred years, although its domed church is a model of Norman Classical architecture. Mondaye houses a community of Cistercians with some forty monks who live a contemplative and apostolic life in the mother-house and in the priories dependant on the abbey.

A lace maker in Bayeux.

A potter in Noron-la-Poterie.

Balleroy Castle.

The Assumption in Mondaye Abbey.

Fontaine-Henry Castle and its very famous roof.

Notre-Dame de la Délivrande.

FONTAINE-HENRY -
A TRADITIONAL
PICTURE
OF NORMANDY

Almost at the gateway to Caen is a steeply-sloping slate roof taller than the building beneath, rising above the surrounding treetops. This is Fontaine-Henry, one of the traditional pictures of Normandy. Built during the Renaissance over the ruins of a fortress, the house has remained in the same family since then, through the female line, and it is still lived in today.

Thaon Church, attractively set in the Mue Valley but unfortunately no longer used for worship, is another example of the perfection of Romanesque architecture in Normandy. The setting is decidedly romantic.

Further north is the basilica church of Notre-Dame-de-la-Délivrande, a model of triumphant Neo-Gothic.

CAEN,
A "POLYPHONIC CITY"

It is the geographical situation of Caen, the capital of Lower Normandy and "county town" of Calvados, at the confluence of the Orne and Odon rivers that has allowed it to expand at ease. The eighteen communities within Greater Caen stretch unrestrainedly into the vast expanse of surrounding countryside without ever really coming to a definite end. The destruction of much of the city in 1944 removed any constraints that the earlier centuries might have placed on the town planners of today. "The long Rue Saint-Jean disappeared without trace because it had been a winding thoroughfare and had been totally destroyed. It was therefore thought simpler to draw out a straight line with a bulldozer," wrote Julien Gracq in his *Carnets du grand voyage.*

Caen is sometimes referred to as the "Athens of Normandy" and is a well-designed, "polyphonic" city according to novelist Didier Decoin. Each passing age has left its mark but has combined it harmoniously with reminders of earlier times. It has also been said that this is the "best reconstructed city in France". The white stone with glints of golden yellow is quarried in the vicinity and has been used for many of the buildings, giving the city a very uniform appearance. Caen may seem to be a city designed according to reason but it is not excessively cold and austere.

Archaeological digs have proved that it existed in Gallo-Roman times, but William the Conqueror and his wife, Matilda, are its real "parents". William had the castle built (it was later extended by his son, Henri) and its massive outline overlooks the picturesque Vaugueux district, the yachting marina and a few streets on the edge of the city centre. From the city walls, there is a panoramic view of the urban thoroughfares and buildings and, within the city, sights include the Exchequer Room which used to be Normandy's seat of justice, St. George's Chapel dating from the 12th Century, the Bailiwick that now houses the Normandy Museum, and the Garden of Medicinal Herbs. The Art Gallery, which has recently been restored and extended, can also be seen there.

Caen owes its two abbeys to William and Matilda. This was the "price" they had to pay in order to obtain the Pope's forgiveness for getting married without his consent when they were very distantly related. Matilda founded Holy Trinity Abbey of which the stocky outline flanked by two towers that unfortunately lost their steeples in the 18th Century rises above the skyline of Caen, almost opposite the castle. Beneath the white vaulting of the fine Romanesque building is the final resting-place of the woman who was Duchess of Normandy and Queen of England but, according to her epitaph, "a pauper among the paupers".

The castle high above Caen, a superb vantage point.

Holy Trinity Abbey, known as the Abbaye-aux-Dames.

The yachting marina in the heart of the town.

St. Stephen's (*abbaye Saint-Etienne*), William's "penance", emphasises the grandeur of the Duke of Normandy who was the future King of England. The two spires flanking the admirable façade rise to a height of 80 metres (260 ft.) above the pavements of Caen and are visible from some distance away across the plain. Building work began in 1066, the year of the Norman conquest of England, and the abbey was inaugurated in 1077. The chancel, chevet, and spires, though, were not completed until the 13th Century, in the Gothic style. The Abbey Church of St. Stephen was restored in the 17th Century using the techniques and designs of its original builders but it bears the marks of many different periods. In front of the altar, beneath a stone slab that seems to be a wager of perennity despite the vicissitudes of history, is all that remains of the abbey's founder — one thigh bone. William's grave was desecrated on several occasions and his bones were scattered far and wide.

In the 17th Century, a monk from Le Bec-Hellouin named William de la Tremblaye, who was an architect and cleric, monitored the reconstruction of the very dilapidated living quarters in both abbeys. This explains the unity of

e Abbaye-aux-Hommes and the abbey buildings which were once used as the Malherbe High School and now house the Town Hall.

The ambulatory in the Abbaye-aux-Hommes.

The Wedding of the Virgin Mary, a painting by Perugino in the Art Gallery.

style. Standing at the end of a vast esplanade decorated with formal gardens is the Abbaye-aux-Hommes (literally, "Men's Abbey") which housed the Malherbe High School after the French Revolution. Nowadays, it is used as the Town Hall and restoration work has given it back its original lustre.

By purchasing the living quarters in the Abbaye-aux-Dames (Women's Abbey), Normandy Regional Council saved them from the destruction for which they were destined. It turned the abbey into its offices and, to do so, not only restored them but also enhanced them. Before entering the great

foyer, the refectory and the lavatorium which are the finest parts of the buildings, there is a superb view of the frontage from the main courtyard.

Caen expanded into a large number of parishes in which the church was the pride and joy of the local population. As a result, it disputes

Old St. Stephen's, a church in ruins.

the title granted to its rival, Rouen, by Victor Hugo of "the town with the one hundred bell-towers". Some of them, such as the old St. Stephen's and St. Giles' Churches were destroyed in 1944 and are now nothing more than a few embryonic pillars on the lawn of a square, like stone arms raised towards the heavens in a search for pity. Others have been rebuilt. St. Peter's (*Saint-Pierre*) whose 78-metre (254 ft.) bell-tower destroyed the nave when it collapsed has regained its Renaissance chevet with the frieze above the arching in the chancel, a veritable Flamboyant Gothic hymn in stone. St. John's (*Saint-Jean*) has even been rebuilt with the inherent imbalance that prevented it from being topped with a steeple and bellcotes when it was first built. Notre-Dame de la Gloriette, with its austere Classical West front, and St. Saviour's (*Saint-*

Sauveur) with its twin chevets and two parallel naves, bear witness to the expansion of Caen at their respective periods in history.

A few old streets have been preserved or restored, including Rue Saint-Pierre, Rue Froide which is linked to a cruel legend, Rue du Moulin, Rue Saint-Sauveur, and Rue du Vaugueux, the symbol of Old Caen although it is, perhaps, rather too colourful. At the foot of the castle is the Quatrans' House. The spaces between its timber beams are filled with red bricks, giving it a fine appearance. The Escoville Residence, which was recently restored by the architect Zninden as a "first step in the architectural discovery of Caen", belonged to one of the city's merchants during the Renaissance.

La Prairie, the hippodrome, and the banks of the R. Orne make Caen a city full of parks, gardens, and open spaces. It is also a town of architectural and historic interest with a lively cultural and social scene and one of the oldest universities in France, founded in 1432 by the Duke of Bedford, Regent of England. Caen is also the twelfth largest harbour in France, linked to the sea by a 15-kilometre (9-mile canal) built in 1850. The city, however, underwent a serious economic crisis when it lost its steelworks, which had been opened on the eve of the First World War by Baron Thyssen. It is hoped that the installation of the national heavy-ion accelerator (the G.A.N.I.L.) at the Institute of Science of Matter and Radiation, like the numerous biomedical and computer research centres, will provide new economic prosperity. Caen, though, which suffered so badly during the war, is also hoping to become known as a city of peace. The Mémorial, on which the long, tall frontage is broken by a single breach symbolising the years of the last world war, is to be the major feature in this vocation.

St. Peter's Church.

Houlgate, the family resort.

FLORAL COAST - REMEMBRANCE OF THINGS PAST

Beyond Merville-Franceville, the popular resort near Caen, is another world just waiting for visitors - the Floral Coast, a synonym of luxury seaside holidays.

Of all the constellation of resorts, Cabourg, Deauville and Trouville are the brightest of the stars, each with its own particular brilliance. Cabourg has the reputation of being the most intellectual of the three, and it steadfastly cultivates memories of one of its earliest visitors, Marcel Proust, who described it in his novels under the name of "Balbec". Deauville, which was founded by the Duke de Morny, is the resort popular with the jet-set

Trouville, a seaside resort and fishing harbour.

A tour of Normandy

The boardwalk in Deauville.

Dives-sur-Mer: Port Guillaume.

and is known as the "21st *arrondissement* of Paris". The casino attracts one million gamblers every year and the race tracks at La Touque and Clairefontaine are more to the taste of the resort's visitors than the beach - its horse races have a larger audience than its regattas. The Grand Prix and sale of yearlings are the main attractions in a season including a whole range of events such as the International American Film Festival. Villas and manor houses, often of very pretentious design and decoration, ensure that "fake Norman" remains as fashionable as ever! Trouville, on the other bank of the R. Touques, is the most popular of the three resorts. Discovered last century by Boudin, Isabey, Daumier etc. the resort has developed without any real town plan, around a fishing harbour which is always full of movement and which is not far from the Louis XIII style casino. In some places, the lack of any structured urban development adds a touch of confusion that gives the resort its own, charming flavour.

Houlgate and Dives-sur-Mer, which lie between the "stars", also have a few aces up their sleeves. Houlgate is a family resort, and the embarkation point for trips to the "Vaches noires" ("Black Cows"), enormous boulders covered in seaweed which fell from the cliffs and are well-known to geologists because of the abundance of fossils they contain.

Dives-sur-Mer emphasises its role as the point at which 696 ships gathered before setting off with William to cross the Channel to

"Especially Balbec, where hotels are already being built..."
(Marcel Proust, Swann's Way).

Pevensey — with the crews and army that were to win the Battle of Hastings. The yachting marina is named after the Conqueror, as is the craft centre housed in a superb 16th-century mansion. British tourists are only too willing to enter Notre-Dame Church where they can read, on a plaque set up there last century, the list of 475 names of knights who accompanied William to Hastings. The 16th-century covered market with its impressive oak rafters is still a bustling place, filled with stalls of all kinds.

The cliffs at Houlgate.

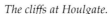

HONFLEUR - A FIRST GLIMPSE OF THE SEA!

Thousands of children have come to Honfleur for their first glimpse of the sea. This is the most easterly port in Calvados, on a stretch of shore known as the Coast of Grace; it is also the nearest port to the "interior".

Binot-Paulmier de Gonneville who sailed to Brazil in 1503, Jean Denis, the first man to explore the Saint-Lawrence Seaway, and Samuel de Champlain who, in 1608, founded Quebec to which so many anonymous Normans travelled after him, all set sail from Honfleur. The town owes much of its heritage to the sea. The entrance to the Old Harbour has been watched over the by Lieutenant's House since the 17th Century. At the foot of Quai Sainte-Catherine, the wind ruffles the reflections of the tall, narrow house fronts and slate roofs that line the quayside. Quai Saint-Etienne provides a contrast to the other wharf, with its luxurious stone houses. There are salt stores here where the valuable commodity used to be kept prior to loading on board the fishing boats that sailed to the banks off Newfoundland.

The organ loft in St. Catherine's Church.

"St. Catherine's Quay reflected in the waters of the old basin"
(Lucie Delarue-Mardrus, L'Ex-Voto).

Then there is St. Catherine's Church built in the 16th Century by ship-wrights in a hurry to have their own church and who built it in the shape of an upturned hull, the form that they were used to assembling day after day.

Honfleur also owes much to the "contemplatives" who came to look at the sea. Hardly a day passed without an artist setting up an easel on its quaysides, jetty, or hills. The first ones came here some one hundred and fifty years ago and the artists of today dream of acquiring the fame and reputation of those who have gone before them such as Boudin, Corot, Lebourg, or Jongkind to name but a few. The meeting-place of all these artists was the Saint-Siméon Farm not far from the town. Nowadays, a fine museum displays a collection of their works and has been named after the first of them all. Honfleur, though, was a favourite with other Muses. It was popular with Musset and Baudelaire etc. and was the birthplace of Erik Satie, Albert Sorel, Henri de Régnier, and Alphonse Allais. As to Lucie Delarue-Mardrus, a somewhat forgotten poet and novelist, she used the town as the subject of her works.

From the town, a hill well-known for its steep slope leads up to the Chapel of Our Lady of Grace. The tiny chapel surrounded by age-old trees was built in the 17th Century after the one erected during the reign of Richard II had been swallowed up by the waves, with the cliffs on which it stood. Beneath the blue-painted vaulted roof decorated with stars, marble engravings bear witness to the close ties between Canada and Normandy and hundreds of votive offerings indicate the gratitude of seafarers to the Blessed Virgin Mary.

THE AUGE AREA - A SEA OF GREENERY DOTTED WITH CASTLES

The Auge area is an out-standing image of lush Normandy, the land of good food, home of cheeses and cider.

The area is fertile and almost obsessively covered in shrubs and vegetation. It is filled with hedgerows and springs and delights not only nature-lovers but also visitors with a passion for pretty villages, superb castles, and elegant manor houses. Crèvecoeur-en-Auge Castle, which lies on the side of the RN 13 road, is one such, and it is a "must" on any tour of western Normandy.

Every guide book and tourist brochure has its own favourite castles and country houses e.g. Canapville, Grandchamp, Coupe-sarte, Bellou, Chiffetot, Saint-Germain de Livet, Victot-Pontfol (it has a famous stud farm), Mont de la Vigne, Fervaques etc.

Bonneville, though, is slightly different to the others. It was once part of a fortress perched on the hillside above the Touques Valley and, from it, there is a breath-taking panoramic view of the entire area. It was here that William made

Crèvecœur-en-Auge.

Saint-Germain de Livet and its checkerboard frontage.

*"Let us pray for the man who planted the apple tree"
(Olivier Basselin).*

preparations for his conquest of England.

Of all the small towns and villages in the Auge area, Beaumont to the north of the A 13 motorway and Beuvron to the south seem to be the most typical. Anybody strolling down the main street in Beuvron might well be tempted to declare, "There's nothing more typical of the Auge area than this". Like so many others, the village seemed doomed to disappear as a result of the rural exodus but an association saved it and rebuilt its houses in the architectural style specific to the area. The covered market which had been demolished shortly before was

also rebuilt, giving back to this real country village the appearance it had several decades ago.

Pont-l'Evêque is the main town in the Auge area and it has made a name for itself thanks to the square, subtly-flavoured cheese that is made here. The town, though, has more than just good food to attract visitors and encourage them to stay awhile. There are its town-houses and its Flamboyant Gothic church. Memories of Flaubert are also rife in its streets and even more in Les Geffosses Farm where he stayed on numerous occasions during his childhood and adolescence.

The former Dominican convent in Pont-l'Evêque.

The village of Beaumont-en-Auge is typical of this area, the birthplace of Laplace.

Pont-l'Evêque cheese has been made since the Middle Ages.

LISIEUX - DESTINY OVERTURNED

Lisieux, a sub-prefecture with a population of 26,000, is the administrative, judicial, commercial and industrial centre of the Auge area. The town made a break with its past history when, in 1889, Thérèse Martin, the daughter of a family who had moved to the town from Alençon only a few years earlier, entered Carmel. Her extraordinary destiny was to turn Lisieux into one of the world's most popular places of pilgrimage, attracting more than two million people every year.

The fire of 1943 left only a few of the half-timbered houses and a small number of private residences standing in the old town of Lisieux. St. Peter's Church (*église Saint-Pierre*), which has a tower flanking the triple portal that has never been completed, was also spared. It was here that the future Carmelite nun used to come and pray as a child.

The fire also spared the former Bishop's Palace which was turned into the courthouse. The "Gilded Drawing Room" is the most outstanding chamber in it.

The destination of most visitors to Lisieux is the Basilica Church of St. Teresa set high above the town on a hillside overlooking the Touques Valley. Built to designs and under the control of architect Louis-Marie Cordonnier, followed by his son and

The basilica.

The reliquary donated by Pope Pius XI.

The "Souterroscope" in Caumont-L'Éventé, a journey of initiation into the Centre of the Earth.

grandson, in a Romanesque-Byzantine style, this is one of the largest churches to have been built in the 20th Century anywhere in the world. It covers an area of 4,500 square metres (48,420 square feet) and has a nave 30 metres (97 ft.) wide. The dome rises to a height of 95 metres (309 ft.) above the esplanade and its campanile, which has never been completed but which contains the great tenor bell, three large bells and a peal of forty-four bells, rises to a height of 45 metres (146 ft.). Its decoration of mosaics made, like the stained-glass windows, by Pierre Gaudin, tells the life story of the young nun and illustrates her message, while at the same time echoing the design of the architecture. One regret that is often heard is that the basilica is the absolute antithesis of the virtues displayed by Thérèse Martin.

A tour of the Carmelite chapel in the town centre where the saint's relics can be seen in a bronze reliquary, followed by a tour of the relics room and Les Buissonets, the house where she lived as an adolescent, give a closer insight into the spirituality and faith that inspired the author of the *Story of a Soul.*

THE CAEN COUNTRYSIDE, WHERE MAN HAS LEFT HIS MARK

Between the Auge region and the pasturelands boxed in by hedgerows is the countryside around Caen and Falaise, a plain almost totally devoid of any geographical features but marked by the struggles, work and genius of mankind.

Set amid lime trees and chestnuts in a park slightly off the Caen

Canon Castle in the middle of its park.

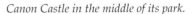

A tour of Normandy

Formal gardens in Vendoeuvre Castle.

to Saint-Pierre-sur-Dives road stands Canon Castle, a reminder of a barrister named Jean-Baptiste Elie de Beaumont who was instrumental in gaining rehabilitation for the Huguenot, Jean Calas, and was one of the enlightened figures of the late 18th Century. The castle was built in the 17th Century. It has a superb white façade and a terrace flanked by an Italianate balustrade, and was considerably extended and embellished by the barrister, who was a close friend of the Encyclopaedists and a great nature-lover. He paid a great deal of attention to the park, commissioning vast quantites of Classical statues and small summer-houses (the Temple of the Weeper, the Mirror of Water, the Chinese Pagoda) which were designed to draw attention to some feature of the house.

Saint-Pierre-sur-Dives can be seen from miles around because of the lantern-tower on its minster. Founded in the 11th Century by Countess Lasceline, the monastery had an eventful history that resul-

The covered market in Saint-Pierre-sur-Dives.

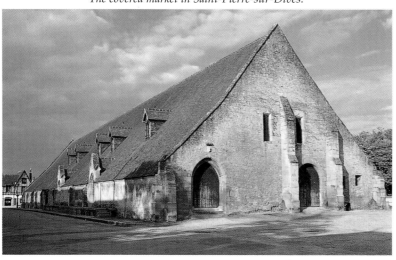

The Talbot Tower in Falaise Castle.

ted in a south tower dating from the 12th Century, a lantern-tower from the 13th, a west front and north tower from the 14th, a 15th-century nave — and modern stained-glass windows.

The abbey buildings now house the Museum of Cheesemaking, which is fairly logical. The town near the abbey has become a major market town and St. Peter's Church is as popular with visitors as its covered market.

Vendoeuvre Castle owes its fame more to its museum than to its 18th-century architecture and formal French-style gardens. Madame de Vendoeuvre, its owner, has patiently collected some five hundred pieces of miniature furniture made over the past four hundred years and has set them out in an exhibition in the Orangery.

FALAISE - LOVE AT FIRST SIGHT IN THE CASTLE

Falaise is one of the major places in the history of Normandy. William the Bastard was born here. At the foot of the castle facing Mont Myrrha, high above the Ante Valley, you can still see the spring where Arlette, the daughter of a local tanner, was washing linen when Robert the Magnificent, son of Richard II, caught sight of her, fell in love and, with her consent, made her his wife "after the Danish fashion". In town, an equestrian statue showing a horseman with lance in hand controlling his tempestuous mount serves as a reminder of the fabulous destiny of the child born to this couple in love.

Tourists today are shown the window from which Robert used to watch Arlette, and the bedroom where she had her child! Yet what really remains of the fortress that was home to the young bastard and his mother until the victory of Val-ès-Dunes near Caen when the felonious barons were defeated? The keep and small keep were not built until after William's death, the former by his son, Henri. The enormous outer wall, which once had fourteen towers (few of them are still standing today), dates from the 13th Century. The Talbot Tower, named after the engineer who designed it, stands 35 metres (114 ft.) high and has walls 4 metres (13 ft.) thick. It dates from the reign of Philip Augustus. Little matter, though, if the troubadours have exaggerated History. Legends are so wonderful when they talk of love.

The town was almost flattened during the battle of the "Falaise pocket" but it has been attractively rebuilt and has more to offer visitors than mere memories of Robert, Arlette and William, fine though these memories may be. The Church of the Holy Trinity (*église de la Trinité*) bears the hallmarks of the Renaissance. St. Gervaise' Church is both Romanesque and Gothic. The churches of St. Lawrence (*Saint-Laurent*) and Notre-Dame-de-

Guibray were probably built at the time of William's birth. The Parizot organ in the second of these two churches, which was installed in the 18th Century, is an absolute masterpiece of craftsmanship.

The former hospital, now the library, the Franciscans' Gate, and La Fresnaye Castle (now an exhibition and leisure centre) are all outstanding examples of vernacular architecture. A few modern buildings (Battle of Falaise Museum, Automaton Museum) have ensured that the 20th Century is included in the town's architectural heritage.

NORMAN ALPS - A MOUNTAIN IN REVERSE

From Putanges-Pont-Ecrepin to Thury-Harcourt, the R. Orne and its tributary, the Rouvrou, have gouged out a deep bed for themselves in a fold of the Armorican Uplands, creating a "mountain in reverse", that a slightly imaginative government minister in the days of the Third Republic described as the "Norman Alps". They spraddle the *départements* of both Orne and Calvados. In the latter, the Clécy cliffs are a favourite haunt of climbers in western France. The river is popular with canoeists while the forests and footpaths attract large numbers of walkers.

Pont d'Ouilly, upstream where the Orne enters Calvados, is the greenest and freshest of small towns. The river forms a waterfall here, and tumbles along its course. Downstream, the iron mine has given Saint-Rémy the colours of an autumnal forest. The Croix de Faverie, Pain de Sucre, and Crêtes are strung out along the chain of hills amid wild surroundings, providing panoramic views.

Thury-Harcourt is an elegant little town set at the place where the Orne flows into the plain. Since the 18th Century, it had had a magnificent castle built for the family that added its name to that of Thury. Unfortunately, the Germans burnt it to the ground in 1944 and, with the exception of its chapel and a few outbuildings, it has remained in ruins ever since. They stand in the middle of 70 hectares of beautifully-tended park and gardens, a tragic and romantic reminder of the past.

"Oh, pretty jolly month of May" (Jean Le Houx, a 16th-century poet from Vire).

Calvados, great pages of history

VIRE, THE HOME OF VAUDEVILLE

Chitterlings from Vire.

Much of the south of Calvados is covered with hedgerows and pastures, creating the type of scenery known as *"bocage"*. Mont Pinçon, which rises to an altitude of 365 metres (1,186 ft.), provides a wonderful panoramic view of the countryside.

Set on a spur of rock above the river that has given the town its name, Vire is the main urban centre in this area. Not far away, the river has gouged out a deep ravine called the Vaux de Vire where fullers, tanners and drapers once worked in large numbers. One of them, Olivier Basselin, a very happy-go-lucky man, used to sing rhyming songs about wine and good food. This is said to be the origin of vaudeville.

The busy town of Condé-sur-Noireau on the edges of Orne and Calvados, was the birthplace of César Dumont d'Urville, a passionate seafarer who founded the land known as the Adélie Coast and helped France to acquire the Venus de Milo.

The nearby Pontecoulant Castle is the most outstanding of the architectural gems in this area. It has belonged to Calvados "county council" since 1908 and contains an exhibition of particularly fine old furniture.

Pontecoulant Castle nestling among the trees.

Orne, a patchwork of forests

The "most noble conquest of man" is still intensively bred in the département of Orne.

From west to east, Orne stretches from the Armorican Upland to the Paris Basin, covering an area of 6,100 square kilometers (2,355 square miles). Normandy's highest hill is to be found here, in the Ecouves Forest where the Signal reaches a height of 417 metres (1,355 ft.). To the north-east, the high hills of the Perche area are filled with streams and rivers.

There are as many fortresses and manor houses, monasteries and churches here as there are in the rest of Normandy. And history has written just as many pages here, the last one being in Chambois on 19th August 1944 when American and Canadian troops met up and cut off the retreat of the 7th German Army. This marked the end of the Battle of Normandy.

Of all the départements in Normandy, Orne is the least densely-populated, with a total of under 300,000 inhabitants. It has no seaboard and is therefore the most rural of them all. At the border, there is a signboard decorated with a pony trotter, a reminder of the area's love of horse breeding — not only trotters but also Percheron draught horses.

There is no doubt that its main attraction is its forest, so come to Orne in the autumn when it is draped in shades of purple and gold.

The remains of the fortress in Domfront.

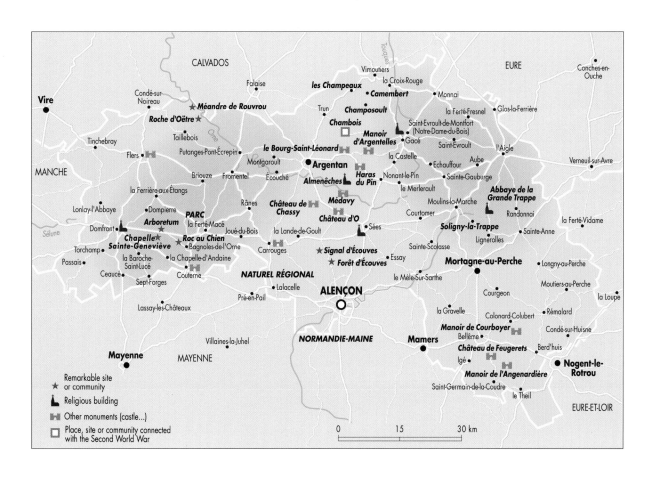

CALVADOS

EURE

Conches-en-Ouche

Falaise

Vire

les Champeaux

la Croix-Rouge

• Camembert

• Monnai

Condé-sur-Noireau

Trun

Champosoult

la Ferté-Fresnel

• Glos-la-Ferrière

★ *Méandre de Rouvrou*

Chambois

Saint-Evroult-de-Montfort

Roche d'Oëtre ★

Manoir d'Argentelles

(Notre-Dame-du-Bois)

Taillebois

• Gacé

Saint-Evroult

l'Aigle

Tinchebray

le Bourg-Saint-Léonard

la Castelle

Putanges-Pont-Écrepin

Verneuil-sur-Avre

Flers

Montgaroult

• Echauffour

Aube

MANCHE

Fromentel

Ecouché

• **Argentan**

Haras du Pin

Nonant-le-Pin

• Sainte-Gauburge

Briouze

Almenêches

le Merlerault

Séluñe

Rânes

Château de Chassy

Médavy

Moulins-la-Marche

Abbaye de la Grande Trappe

la Ferré-aux-Étangs

Lonlay-l'Abbaye

• Dompierre

PARC

Château d'O

Courtomer

Randonnai

la Ferté-Vidame

Arboretum ★

la Ferté-Macé

Joué-du-Bois

la Lande-de-Goult

• Sées

Domfront

Chapelle Sainte-Geneviève ★

Roc au Chien ★

Soligny-la-Trappe

Sainte-Anne

• Bagnoles-de-l'Orne

Lignerolles

Torchamp

la Chapelle-d'Andaine

Carrouges

★ *Signal d'Écouves*

Sainte-Scolasse

Mortagne-au-Perche

• Longny-au-Perche

la Baroche-Saint-Lucé

★ *Forêt d'Écouves*

• Essay

Passais

Couterne

Moutiers-au-Perche

Ceaucé

Sept-Forges

NATUREL RÉGIONAL

le Mêle-Sur-Sarthe

la Loupe

Courgeon

• Lalacelle

ALENÇON

la Gravelle

Pré-en-Pail

○

Colonard-Colubert

• Rémalard

Condé-sur-Huisne

Lassay-les-Châteaux

Manoir de Courboyer

Villaines-la-Juhel

NORMANDIE-MAINE

Mamers

Château de Feugerets

Berd'huis

Mayenne

MAYENNE

Igé

• **Nogent-le-Rotrou**

Bellême

Manoir de l'Angenardière

Saint-Germain-de-la-Coudre

le Theil

EURE-ET-LOIR

★ Remarkable site or community

Religious building

Other monuments (castle...)

□ Place, site or community connected with the Second World War

0   15   30 km

THE PASSAIS AREA - WAR AND PEACE BENEATH THE PEAR TREES

Domfront is the main town in the Passais area, a place with character where apple trees give way to pears and cider is replaced by perry. It is also a very fine introduction to Orne. Standing 70 metres (228 ft.) above the Varenne Gorge, the town provides an extensive panoramic view of the surrounding area.

It was Sully, one of Henri IV's ministers, who had the fortress demolished, a fortress which kings of France and England in turn had attacked. All that remains today, in the middle of a public park, is the keep, a few stones from the outer wall, a number of lookout posts, and, also in ruins, St. Symphorian's Chapel.

All along the streets leading to the Church of St. Julian, an amazing construction in the Neo-Byzantine style with a traceried reinforced cement bell-tower, are a few half-timbered houses and private residences, providing one last reminder of the distant past.

The church in the priory of Notre-Dame-sur-l'Eau.

A fresco in St. Julian's Church.

The Church of Our Lady on the Water (*église Notre-Dame-sur-l'Eau*) on the banks of the Varenne was a priory of the nearby Lonlay Abbey. It suffered some damage during the last war but has been restored. The damage inflicted on it in the 19th Century, however, was irremediable. It lost seven bays to leave space for the road.

BAGNOLES,
THE SPA TOWN WITH A KICK

Bagnoles-de-l'Orne stands in the middle of 4,000 hectares of woodland (the Andaines Forest) and developed as the result of a legend. "Rapide", an old charger that had been abandoned by the Lord of Tessé jumped into a spring and returned to the stables, frisky as a colt. His master also bathed in the spring, followed by a monk, and both regained their youthful vigour. The story spread far and wide and, soon, thousands of sick people came to seek a cure for their ills in the waters.

Nowadays, the mineral water, which has a fairly high radioactive content, is used to treat blood circulation disorders, problems of the endocrinal system and sequels to fractures. The 20,000 people who come here every year to take the waters are, like the ordinary visitors, always delighted by the setting and the somewhat old-fashioned atmosphere common to many a spa town. From the lake, where the ruffled waters give a trembling reflection of the casino, people here for treatment can walk along the Allée du Dante to the pump rooms or go for a walk in the park. Some may even go as far as Tessée-la-Madeleine, the town linked to Bagnoles for the purposes of exploiting the mineral spring, where the old castle has become the Town Hall. From the promontory known as Dog's Rock (Roc au Chien) on the edge of the park planted with giant redwoods, there is a delightful view. Legend has it that, in days gone by, a dog would devour any young girls of marriageable age who ventured to this spot.

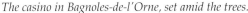

The casino in Bagnoles-de-l'Orne, set amid the trees.

The inner courtyard in Carrouges Castle.

CARROUGES,
A DARK LEGEND

Is it because of the forest? Legends are rife here, some joyful, others foul indeed. There is one about the "Bonvouloir Lighthouse", the tower on a castle that is nearly totally ruined. Its phallic shape is said to have been ordered by the local nobleman who was delighted to have regained his virility after bathing in the waters of the Great Spring.

Beyond La Ferté-Macé on the Alençon road stands Carrouges Castle, one of the best-known castles in Normandy. Built in the middle of a 7-hectare park and sur-rounded by a moat, it combines the Henri IV and Louis XIII styles, and its mixed military and vernacular appearance produces an overall impression of severity and austerity. The barbican looks more elegant, one might almost say more "welcoming", with its red and black diamond-shaped brick ornamentation, its ornate bay in a tall slate roof, and the two turrets to each side.

This country house, though, is steeped in tragic legend. While pregnant, the Countess of Carrouges discovered her husband, Ralph, in the arms of his mistress and stabbed her to death. The murder victim, however, was a fairy and she wreaked terrible revenge. Ralph was found murdered the next day. When the Countess was told the news, a red spot appeared in the middle of her forehead and, a few months after his birth, her son also acquired the same mark. He was known thereafter as Karl the Red, i.e. Karl le Rouge or Carrouges. The malediction continued to the seventh generation.

Carrouges Castle was given to the French National Trust

60

(*Monuments Historiques*) on the eve of the last war by the Le Veneur-Tillières who had been its owners since the reign of Louis XI. It now houses the head offices of the Normandy-Maine Regional Country Park, an area of 234,000 hectares containing one hundred and fifty-one towns and villages in Orne, Manche, Mayenne and Sarthe.

Flers Castle, the headquarters of royalist leader Louis de Frotté.
It now houses the Town Hall and
a museum of art and heritage.

LA ROCHE-D'OETRE, A NORMAN "ABYSS"

The Norman Alps nose into the area around Flers and Argentan. These are the same "Alps" that visitors have already seen in Calvados. Some of their finest beauty spots, however, lie within Orne, including the Saint-Aubert Gorge and the meander of the R. Rouvrou. The cliff that forms the Oetre Rock is over three hundred feet high and shaped like a human face. It looks superbly down over the Rouvre as its waters flow beneath the trees in the direction of the R. Orne. The top of the rock is only a few steps from the road but anybody walking along the edge of this "Norman abyss" should take particular care.

THE ARGENTAN AREA, THE END OF A BATTLE

Argentan lies at the confluence of the rivers Ure and Orne. It is a sub-prefecture of 18,000 people and is a mainly industrial town. In the days of Colbert , and up to the present time, it was a major lace producer, like Alençon. Nowadays, only the Benedictine nuns of Notre-Dame still produce the needlepoint lace that looks like a honeycomb.

As far as architectural heritage is concerned, the town has an impressive 14th-century castle which now houses the law courts, the "Flamboyant Gothic" and Renaissance Church of St. Germain and St. Martin, and St. Nicholas Chapel that has been deconsecrated and now contains the tourist office and municipal library.

The town of Chambois near Argentan is famous among historians — and among specialists in military architecture. It was at the foot of the awesome keep (or very nearly so) and its four towers built in the mid 12th Century that Canadian and Polish soldiers from the north met up with American and French soldiers from the west on 19th August 1944. This placed the 7th German Army in a pincer grip and very few German divisions were able to escape. Three days later, their military chiefs capitulated in the neighbouring village of Tournai-sur-Dives.

Medavy.

A TOUR OF THE CASTLES

The country roads that run from Chambois down to Alençon form one of the finest areas for touring in the whole of Orne and there are plenty of stops along the way. Bourg Saint-Léonard to visit the castle. Argentelles for its fortress-like manor house. Exmes, once the main town in the Hiemois area, to enjoy the panoramic view. Almenèches for its Renaissance church and the terra cotta statues illustrating the life of St. Opportune. Medavy where three castles were built in turn on the same site, each retaining something of its predecessor. And Mortrée, of course, for the Château d'O, one of the most attractive country houses in Normandy. It has brick and stone checkerboard bonding on the façades, tall carved windows, pepperpot towers, and a steeply-sloping roof, all features that underline its ethereal quality and its elegance. Built in the 16th Century, the castle has undergone frequent alterations since then. Its most illustrious owner was François d'O, Intendant of Finance and "favourite" of Henri III. Most of the embellishments date from his period of ownership and were paid for - by the State.

Argentan Castle, now the Law Courts.

Château d'O, one of Normandy's finest country houses.

LE PIN,
A VERSAILLES FOR HORSES

Along this same winding, twisting route is one of the most popular sights in Orne, known to all horse-lovers - Le Pin. The stud that has brought fame to the small town stands in a quite outstanding setting.

The stud farm at Le Pin.

There are 1,000 hectares of meadows, park and gardens laid out by Le Nôtre. The castle itself was designed by Jules Hardouin-Mansart. It houses the managerial offices and the stud's reception rooms and is as lavish as the exterior. People wanted something large and beautiful in the days of Colbert, who introduced the idea of studs in 1665 in an effort to limit the imports of horses. Le Pin was built between 1715 and 1730. It almost disappeared during the French Revolution when studs were closed down but the revolutionaries quickly realised their mistake and the horses were brought back to this equestrian Versailles. Nowadays,

eighty stallions of all breeds live in the lap of luxury here.

Saint-Christophe-le-Jajolet is the site of a pilgrimage to the patron saint of car drivers; it is also the location of Sassy Castle, which was built in the 18th and 19th Centuries at the top of three rows of gardens and terraces.

Beyond it, stretching southwards, are the 14,000 hectares of the Ecouves Forest. It is a forest of oaks and beeches and, as such, it provides beechnuts and acorns for the many stags, roe and fallow deer in its copses. Normandy's highest peak lies within the forest — the Signal d'Ecouves.

A tour of Normandy

ALENÇON,
THE DISCRETION AND
CHARM OF LACE

The charms of Alençon may not be apparent at first sight. Its suburbs are as banal as the outskirts of other towns. Its architectural treasures are scattered. The Corn Market, a huge stone rotunda topped with a glass dome built during the days of the Empire may be one of the sights but it suggests that Alençon is an austere place and this is very far from the truth.

Of the castle built by the Counts and Dukes of Bellême in the 14th and 15th Centuries, Henri IV left nothing but the section that, during the Napoleonic Empire, was turned into the *département's* remand centre. It is from the outside that the enormous towers at the entrance and the domed tower are best seen, and they give some idea of the size of the original building. The Town Hall is a lavish curving stone building dating from the late 18th Century. It stands on the site within the walls that was once occupied by the Summer Palace.

Further south, in the St. Leonard district, is the more mediaeval town of Alençon.

On the north side, the *préfecture* (county buildings) and *Département* Centre have their offices in the former Intendant's Residence, better-known as the Guise Mansion. Opposite it is the birthplace of St. Teresa of the Child Jesus.

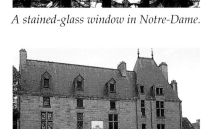
A stained-glass window in Notre-Dame.

The Ozé House.

The Corn Market, now an arts centre.

The Trade Court is housed in the former Exchequer, described by Balzac as the "Cabinet of Antiquities". The tourist office occupies the Ozé Residence.

Notre-Dame Church in the main street suffers from a lack of space and it is difficult to see it from a good angle. It, too, has a pepperpot bell-tower which gives it a heavy outline. On the other hand, there is plenty of room to admire the superb west front with its three porches. The nave and side aisles are built in a light Gothic style that contrasts with the majestic Classicism of the apse and transept. If you visit the church on a sunny day, you will be able to appreciate the full beauty of the eleven Renaissance stained-glass windows that let light into the building.

Alençon is famous for its lace. A museum housed in a former Jesuit college that has been beautifully restored retraces the history of the craft and includes an exhibition of several masterpieces. It was Colbert who made the fortune of Alençon lace which was first designed by Madame de La Perrière. In 1665, he set up the Royal Alençon Laceworks and its output soon outstripped the production from elsewhere. It is made with needles with no backing and without the use of any machinery whatsoever, and is extremely intricate. Even the smallest piece takes hours to make. A few workers in the National Alençon Lace Workshop are continuing the traditional production today. The college houses the Art Gallery, as well as the lace museum.

SÉES, A RELIGIOUS CAPITAL

The main town in Orne left the seat of the bishopric to Sées. And it is true that the capital of the former duchy has never contested it. After all, the bishopric dates back to the year 400 A.D! The town in which the stonework and architecture form an introduction to the nearby Paris Basin is steeped in a fairly unusual atmosphere of tranquillity and meditation, especially as there are numerous religious communities living in the shadow of the bishop's palace. The cathedral is the finest building in Sées, although the piers that had to be added to its west front in the 16th Century to provide additional support spoil the beauty of its outline. The nave, transept and chancel, on the other hand, have retained the pure Norman Gothic lines of the original building.

The former Bishop's Palace, the Church of Notre-Dame-de-la-Place, St. Martin's Abbey lodgings, and the *département's* Museum of Religious Art underline the fact that Sées is very much a religious town.

Sées: the cathedral. Opposite: *Notre-Dame de Sées.*

Bellême, once a fortress and now a magnificent vantage point.

THE PERCHE AREA, "A PROVINCIAL AREA WITH CHARACTER"

There are vast oak and beech forests here dotted with mysterious lakes, and every nook and cranny is well-known to mushroom gatherers. There are the equally endless pastures and, on the horizon, the enormous blue-tinted swell of hills. This is the Perche area, the "provincial area with character" as Alain described it.

Bellême in the south provides a breathtaking view of the area as a whole. Built on a rise at the end of a long avenue, the town was a fortress which was subjected to many a siege, including one led by Blanche of Castile and her son, the future St. Louis.

Its forest, crossed by the RD 938 road, is one of the most outstanding stretches of woodland in Western France. A few castles and manor houses, or in some instances mere fortified farmsteads, most of them built in the 15th and 16th Centuries, come as a delightful surprise when seen from a bend in the road. They include Les Feugerets, l'Angenardière, Courboyer etc.

Mortagne-au-Perche is the subprefecture with a population of scarcely 5,000. Its administrative

"(...) The geographer said we have pointed roofs because it often rains in Normandy," wrote Alain whose house in Mortagne, which once belonged to the Counts of Le Perche, now contains the museum.

role has given it a somewhat severe air which is quickly forgotten once past the St. Dennis Gate.

The buildings above the arcades house the Perche Museum and the nearby House of the Counts of Perche contains the Alain Museum, named after the author who was the most famous of all the town's sons, Emile Chartier. He was a moralist and philosopher born in a house only a short distance away but which is difficult to find and he liked to say, "I am from Perche. That means I am something other than a Norman." This is a fairly dense urban environment but Notre-Dame is worth a visit, arguably rather more for its decoration than for its architecture. Like many parish churches, it benefited from the clearing of abbey churches, in this instance the church in the Charterhouse of Valdieu. Mortagne acquired the apsidal altar, the choir stalls, and the pulpit, all of them made in the 18th Century. One of the stained-glass windows recalls the major role played by Pierre Boucher and other local people in the founding of Canada.

Of the 18th-century mansions, one is now the Town Hall and another the Sub-Prefecture. "Henri IV's House" is older and the monarch is said to have slept here. It has to be said that the king was as popular as he was a great sleeper. The cloisters in the old St. Francis Convent (*couvent Saint-François*) and the crypt in St. Andrew's Church (*église Saint-André*) are other parts of the architectural heritage in Mortagne-au-Perche where, strangely enough, there are large numbers of sundials decorating the house fronts.

A tour of Normandy

FROM PERCHE TO OUCHE - FORESTS AND ABBEYS

To the north of Mortagne, the hills of the Perche area become higher, reaching 309 metres (1,004 ft.) in the Monts d'Amain, and 303 metres (985 ft.) in Lignerolles in the Perche State Forest where they run into the rugged Ouche area. Beneath the trees covering an area of almost 3,000 hectares near Chaumont Lake, stands the Trappist monastery called the Grande Trappe de Soligny, jealously guarding its silence.

The only town of any size in this area is L'Aigle, which gets its name from a bird of prey's nest said to have been found there in the 12th Century. St. Martin's Church is the most outstanding building in the town. It stands on the hillside overlooking the Risle Valley.

Les Nouettes, not far from L'Aigle, will remind French people of the tales they were told as children. The castle was the home of the Comtesse de Ségur, author of the "Sophie" series. A museum in Aube contains memorabilia concerning the countess and her family.

THE LAND OF CAMEMBERT...

Before returning to Eure and Upper Normandy, the tour of Orne ends with a trip back into the Auge area. In Vimoutiers, a peaceful little town on the banks of the R. Vie which also suffered during the war, the memory lives on of Marie Harel, a name that should be known to gourmets and gourmands alike. She was a farmer's wife in Camembert (or, some say, in Champosoult) and is said to have been the inventor of Camembert cheese. In Vimoutiers, the statue of the farmer's wife was paid for by an American cheesemaker.

In Champeaux, another village on the edge of the Auge area, the person whose birthplace is open to the public is part of the history of France itself. She was Charlotte Corday, a grand-niece many times removed of dramatist Pierre Corneille and it was she who murdered Marat, the friend of the people, as a result of her Republican ideals.

The Grande Trappe in Soligny, an abbey founded by the Benedictines in the 12th Century but reformed by Father de Rancé in the 17th.

Eure,
a summary of the entire province

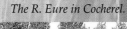

The R. Eure rises in the Perche area and flows into the Seine at Pont-de-l'Arche after covering a distance of 235 kilometres (146 miles) and it has given its name to one of the two *départements* in Upper Normandy.

The 520,000 inhabitants in this *département* sometimes feel as if they are the Cinderellas of Upper Normandy despite the fact that Eure is undergoing a population explosion that is not echoed in Seine-Maritime. Eure is a rural, farming area to the west but industrial to the east and it has a short, but no less real, shoreline. It suffers, though, from the attraction of Paris (or perhaps it actually benefits from it) and is yet another one of the

The tower on the Church of St. Mary Magdalen in Verneuil-sur-Avre. Built in the 15th and 16th Centuries, it stands 56 metres - 182 ft. high, and is often compared to the Butter Tower in Rouen Cathedral.

The R. Eure in Cocherel.

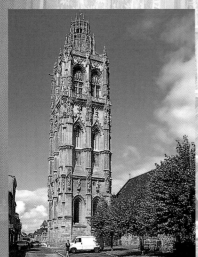

A tour of Normandy

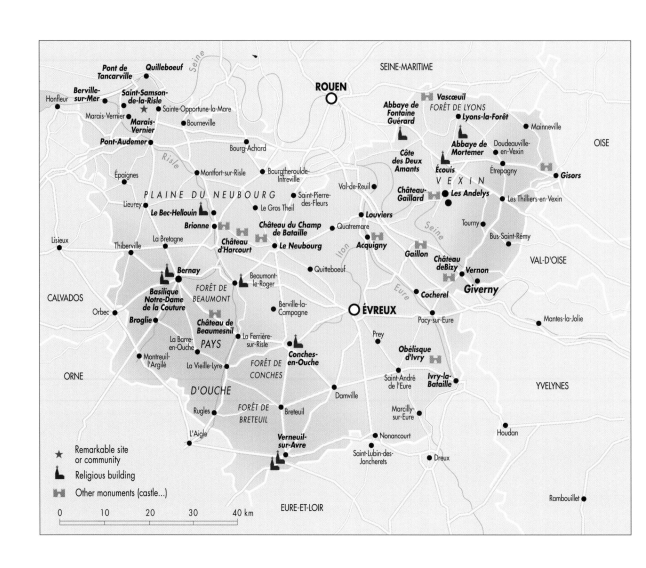

SEINE-MARITIME

ROUEN

Pont de Tancarville
Quilleboeuf
Saint-Samson-de-la-Risle
Sainte-Opportune-la-Mare
Berville-sur-Mer
Honfleur
Marais-Vernier
Marais-Vernier
Bourneville
Pont-Audemer
Bourg-Achard

Vascœuil
Abbaye de Fontaine Guérard
FORÊT DE LYONS
Lyons-la-Forêt
Mainneville
Côte des Deux Amants
Abbaye de Mortemer
Doudeauville-en-Vexin
Écouis
Étrepagny
Gisors
OISE

Épaignes
Montfort-sur-Risle
Bourgtheroulde-Infreville
Val-de-Reuil
V E X I N
PLAINE DU NEUBOURG
Saint-Pierre-des-Fleurs
Château-Gaillard
Les Andelys
Les Thilliers-en-Vexin
Lieurey
Le Gros Theil
Le Bec-Hellouin
Louviers
Tourny
Brionne
Quatremare
Bus-Saint-Rémy
La Bretagne
Château du Champ de Bataille
Risle
Château d'Harcourt
Le Neubourg
Acquigny
Seine
Lisieux
Thiberville
Gaillon
Château deBizy
Vernon
VAL-D'OISE
Beaumont-le-Roger
Quitteboeuf
Iton
Giverny
CALVADOS
Bernay
FORÊT DE BEAUMONT
Cocherel
Orbec
Basilique Notre-Dame de la Couture
Berville-la-Campagne
ÉVREUX
Orbec
Pacy-sur-Eure
Mantes-la-Jolie
Broglie
Château de Beaumesnil
La Ferrière-sur-Risle
Prey
Eure
La Barre-en-Ouche
PAYS
Obélisque d'Ivry
Montreuil-l'Argilé
La Vieille-Lyre
FORÊT DE CONCHES
Conches-en-Ouche
Saint-André de l'Eure
Ivry-la-Bataille
YVELYNES
ORNE
Damville
D'OUCHE
Marcilly-sur-Eure
Houdan
Rugles
FORÊT DE BRETEUIL
Breteuil
L'Aigle
Verneuil-sur-Avre
Nonancourt
Dreux
Saint-Lubin-des-Joncherets
Rambouillet

★ Remarkable site or community

⌂ Religious building

▥ Other monuments (castle...)

EURE-ET-LOIR

0   10   20   30   40 km

départements which has so many different faces. Indeed, individual areas such as Ouche or Vexin have a stronger identity than the *département* as a whole. The engines used in the Ariane rocket are manufactured here, and people still ride to hounds. The writer, Jean de La Varende, who lived in Chamblac Castle near Bernay, said that Eure on its own summed up the whole of Normandy, a province which he knew intimately and which he loved.

Hauville Mill in the Brotonne Regional Park.

Le Val-Gallerand Farm in Grosley-sur-Risle.

Timbered houses in Pont-Audemer.

THE VERNIER MARSHES, "OF A GREEN SO BEAUTIFUL..."

Before flowing into the sea, the Seine has dug out a marshy plain in the Roumois Plateau, a sort of amphitheatre in which its course forms the stage. These are the Vernier Marshes.

The Vernier Marshes face the highly-industrialised right bank of the Seine but have remained an unparalleled area of natural beauty even if an occasional whiff of petrol blows over them and if the night sky is set ablaze by the flash of the flares. From the Saint-Samson-de-la-Roque Lighthouse or the viewing table on the Côte Pelée, they can be seen in their entirety with their checkerboard layout of canals, rows of white poplars, and great lake. On a stone, an inscription praises the grass and Normandy, "Of a green so beautiful that even Hope can dream".

The villages of Quilleboeuf, Le Marais Vernier, and Sainte-Opportune, the cottages with their gardens spiked with irises, the indigenous flora and fauna (ducks, herons, Highland cows, Camargue horses) all attract visitors and encourage them to stay awhile.

A trip up the R. Risle, a coastal river that rises in Orne and joins the Seine Estuary near Berville-sur-Mer to the west of the marshes is even more attractive on a fine June evening or a clear autumn afternoon.

Pont-Audemer was made prosperous by tanners and papermakers. It has earned itself the nickname of "the Venice of Normandy".

LE BEC, THE KNIGHT AND THE MONK!

Further upstream is a square tower topped by a balustrade and a pinnacle, in a small valley leading to the banks of the R. Risle. It signals Le Bec-Hellouin, one of the most outstanding sightseeing venues in Normandy. Known as the St. Nicholas Tower and built in the 15th Century, this is the only substantial remainder of the minster of the famous monastery. Le Bec-Hellouin Abbey was almost on a par with Mont Saint-Michel (in the Normandy dialect, a "bec" is a stream, or beck) and, in the Middle Ages or again in the 17th Century, it had an intense intellectual and spiritual influence on the Church. The French Revolution sounded its death knoll. During the Napoleonic Empire, the monastery buildings were turned into a prison then, later, into a remount depot. The abbey was not brought back to life again until 1948. The Benedictines who returned to set up a new community gave it back its initial purpose as a place of prayer, study, and retreat for anybody in search of such things and made it a centre of spiritual and intellectual exchange attracting people from all over the world.

The abbey was originally founded by a former knight, Herluin, and by a monk from Milan named Lanfranc. From 1093 onwards, another Italian monk, St. Anselme, continued its work and Le Bec gave England many of its archbishops and abbots. There is a plaque inside the monastery to remind visitors of this fact and another plaque that maintains the links between the abbey and the University of Cambridge.

The St. Nicholas Tower in Le Bec-Hellouin.

In the 17th Century, a cleric left the abbey where he had taken his vows in 1669. He was Guillaume de la Tremblaye who served God through his talents as an architect and through his daring designs. Before leaving Le Bec for Caen (we have already mentioned him in connection with the city), he designed the cloisters reached by the matins staircase, one of the few parts of the abbey to have been spared during the French Revolution.

Another area that escaped destruction was the refectory, built in the 18th Century. It became the new minster. Near the high altar, a gift from the people of the Italian town of Aosta is the sarcophagus containing the body of Herluin, the knight who gave Normandy not the glory that goes with feats of bravery on the battlefield but the glory that comes from faith and spirituality.

The Abbey of Le Bec-Hellouin.

BERNAY,
A NORMAN-BRETON ALLIANCE

Bernay developed around the abbey founded by Richard II and his wife, Judith of Brittany, and was the birthplace of the author of the *Roman d'Alexandre* and inventor of the alexandrine, the solemn verse form with twelve feet. It was also the birthplace of members of the National Convention, Robert and Thomas Lindet. During the French Revolution, the town became a sub-prefecture and it has remained so ever since. It is a lively town, full of shops, and although it has a population of only just 11,000, it has its own charm and character.

The minster commissioned in 1013 by William of Volpiano, Abbot of Fécamp, is a wonderful example of primitive Romanesque architecture. It was taken back from the State which had been using it as a store and underwent wide-ranging renovation. The Abbot's lodgings dating from the 16th Century now house a museum and the monks' living quarters dating from the 17th Century

Old houses in Bernay.

A gravestone in Sainte-Croix.

are now the Town Hall. Holyrood Church (*église Sainte-Croix*) at the start of Rue Thiers, has undergone a number of alterations since the 15th Century and has acquired several works of art from Le Bec-Hellouin including the high altar, gravestones, statues of the twelve Apostles etc. The network of narrow streets contains a few half-timbered houses whose façades, foundations or gardens are lapped by the waters of the rivers Charentonne or Cosnier.

Built in the 15th Century in another district of the town, indeed in an area that is almost a totally different Bernay altogether, is Notre-Dame-de-la-Couture, which has timber vaulting and superb stained-glass windows. It was raised to the status of basilica in 1950. Every year on Whit Monday, the brotherhoods of charity in Normandy all gather here for a pilgrimage in honour of Notre-Dame-de-la-Couture.

Ten kilometres (six miles) upstream from Bernay is the small town of Broglie, named after a famous Italian family which settled here in the 18th Century and gave France the renowned physicists, Maurice and Louis de Broglie.

THE OUCHE AREA, HOME OF LA VARENDE

The right bank of the R. Charentonne marks the end of the "immense Ouche Plateau" as Jean de La Varende described it. He drew on this area for the subject matter of many of his stories and novels. The writer lived locally, in Bonneville Castle in Chamblac where he is buried. Between Eure and Orne, the countryside is austere, a land of meadows, scrubby woodland or opulent

Beaumesnil Castle. "Nowhere in France is there a Louis XIII residence of such beauty," said La Varende.

forests such as Beaumont-le-Roger, Breteuil or Conches. Iron ore used to provide the raw material for the metalworking industry in days gone by. The industry has now died out.

Beaumesnil Castle on the plateau is unanimously considered as one of the most outstanding country houses in Normandy. Built between 1633 and 1640, it is a masterpiece of the Louis XIII style. It belongs to the Jean Furstenberg Foundation named after the art critic who last purchased it and houses a number of priceless collections from the National Library. It also has a bookbinding museum.

Conches, in the north of the Ouches area, has a statue of a wild boar on its main square. It stands at the foot of a ruined keep.

The main sight in Conches, though, is the stained glass in St. Faith's Church (*église Sainte-Foy*). The tall nave and spire rise high above the scarp slope with the R. Rouloir flowing past its foot. The stained glass in the chancel was inspired by the works of Dürer, Aldegraver and other German engravers and depicts scenes from the New Testament, and the martyrdom of St. Faith, a young Christian girl whose relics were brought back from Conques in Aquitaine by Roger de Tosny, the first Lord of Conches. The windows date from the 16th Century and are thought to be the work of Romain Buron, a pupil of the master glasspainter from Beauvais, Engrand Le Prince. The windows in the side aisles, which are older, depict the life of the Virgin Mary (south aisle). The finest of them all, in the north aisle, illustrates the "mystic wine-press", symbolising the mystery of the Eucharist.

Stained-glass windows in St. Faith's Church (église Sainte-Foy).

VERNEUIL-SUR-AVRE, "NEVER CLOSED"!

Is Verneuil-sur-Avre really part of the Ouche area? History and geography are at odds in this respect. Was it not, after all, the capital of the "French lands"?

The eye that is the town's emblem tops the motto "Never closed" and this clearly states the town's purpose as a border community.

A 15th-century house in Verneuil-sur-Avre.

In addition to the reminders of an eventful mediaeval period, Verneuil has some superb timbered or stone houses but its most outstanding sights are two wonderful churches. The belfry beside the Church of Mary Magdalen (*église de la Madeleine*), which is 56 metres (182 ft.) high and built in the Flamboyant Gothic style, has often been compared to the Butter Tower or, in some cases, deemed to be aesthetically superior to it. Inside, a cenotaph by David d'Angers keeps alive the memory of royalist rebel Louis de Frotté and his companions, who were shot by firing squad in Verneuil on the orders of Bonaparte. The Church of Mary Magdalen and Notre-Dame Church are to statues what Conches is to stained glass. There are monochrome and polychrome statues made of stone or wood, the finest of them in the Church of Mary Magdalen being the "Virgin Mary with the Apple" and the Entombment of Christ. In Notre-Dame, the most outstanding statues depict St. Dennis, St. James, St. Christopher and a Virgin Mary Lamenting, showing the perfection achieved between the 13th and 16th Centuries by the sculptors of the Verneuil School in the art of expressing in a face or in body movement feelings such as joy or suffering, indeed the whole gamut of human sentiment.

EVREUX, A CATHEDRAL ON THE BANKS OF THE ITON

The Iton is a tributary of the Eure and it gives Evreux, the "county town", much of its charm as its waters branch off to form several different streams. In the centre, it laps against the walls of the Gallo-Roman and mediaeval town. Its banks have been laid out with delightful promenades that provide magnificent views of the cathedral.

Of all the historic buildings in the bishopric, this is the most out-

Notre-Dame Cathedral in Evreux.

St. Taurin's reliquary.

*A stained-glass window in the
Lady Chapel in the cathedral.*

The belfry.

standing. Like Evreux itself, the cathedral has been destroyed and rebuilt on many occasions. Its monumental majesty is best seen when it juts up from the shadows, picked out from the surrounding darkness by the floodlights. The finest view is from the hillsides of Saint-Michel. During the day, take time to admire its nave, side aisles, chancel and apsidal chapels. Its windows, especially in the chancel where they date from the 14th Century, the wooden screens in the side chapels, and the wrought-iron grilles in the chancel are just some of the decorative features that reflect the grandeur of the architecture.

The church dedicated to St. Taurin, the first Bishop of Evreux, is more modest. It was built in the 14th and 15th Centuries. In addition to its superb stained-glass windows, it has a gilded silver reliquary containing St. Taurin's relics which was given to the town by St. Louis. It is a masterpiece of 13th-century goldsmithing.

The former bishop's palace has been turned into a museum with a range of different collections. The section devoted to archaeology in Eure is of particular interest.

The Town Hall, belfry, theatre, and art gallery are all concentrated within a small area of the town centre, forming a set of buildings with a diversity that is far from unattractive.

Harcourt Castle...

NEUBOURG PLAIN - STRETCHING TO THE HORIZON

The Neubourg Plain stretches westwards, as far as the eye can see.

Its main town, Le Neubourg, is somehow reminiscent of the plain. Its square is so vast that the parish church of St. Peter and St. Paul seems to get lost on it. Only the Wednesday market, a real Norman market full of colour, exciting smells, and lots of noise, makes the square seem too small. A castle once stood on this spot. It took four centuries to build but it was demolished in 1785 except for one half-timbered section, the Knights' Chamber and a few sections that can be seen from the suburbs.

Vitotel Church not far away is a tiny flint building with limestone bonding set in a meadow.

Its simplicity forms a sharp contrast to the luxury of Battlefield Castle (Château du Champ de Bataille). Built in the late 17th Century for Alexandre de Crequi, the huge house has two wings flanking central apartments.

Its neighbour, Harcourt Castle, is quite different. It is an awesome fortress, a masterpiece of military architecture hidden among the undergrowth. Harcourt is as popular for its arboretum containing more than 200 varieties of rare tropical trees as it is for the castle.

And Battlefield Castle…

THE RIVER EURE - WAR AND PEACE!

Some 15 kilometres (9 miles) east of the main town, the R. Eure glides lazily through a fairly wide valley in which the hillsides were, for many years, covered in vines. Yet peaceful though they may appear, they sometimes resounded to the clash of arms.

Ivry entered the history books in the wake of Henri IV's "white plume". A few miles away is an obelisk serving as a reminder of his victory over the Duke of Mayenne, commander-in-chief of the Leaguers.

Cocherel, downstream, is a village in which history showed bitter irony. In 1364, Du Guesclin routed Charles the Bad's troops here. A pyramid in the plain is a memorial to his victory. In more recent times, Cocherel was the favourite place of residence of Aristide Briand and the "Apostle of Peace" is buried in the graveyard beside the church. Near the bridge across the river, there is a commemorative statue of the politician but just a few yards further on is a plaque indicating that his efforts were in vain — it commemorates the fighting that took place here in June 1940.

"And he delivered Jesus to their will"
(Luke 23) - Notre-Dame Church in Louviers

LOUVIERS AND ITS LINEN-DRAPERS

Louviers "the Frank" is the third largest town in Eure and it has played a major role in the history of Normandy.

By the 13th Century, Louviers had already acquired a reputation as a cloth-making town and it maintained it quite brilliantly until the middle of the 19th Century. The R. Eure, which split into a large number of separate streams here, was navigable at that time and its waters also powered the factories and workshops. A stained-glass window in Notre-Dame Church recalls the work of the linen drapers. A few old houses, the ruins of the Penitents' convent including cloisters with an almost unique design that stand on an arm of the river, and the wonderful promenade along the river bank constitute the town's attractions. It is, though, Notre-Dame Church that takes the longest visit. It underwent extensive alteration in the 15th Century and its side is now a magnificent example of Flamboyant Gothic architecture. Of the porch, somebody once wrote that it was a "masterpiece of goldsmithing rather than a stonemason's construction". The 14th and 16th-century statues are also very ornate.

Louviers suffered badly during the last war but it is proud to count among its past mayors Pierre Mendès-France.

The Wakhevicht Foundation is housed in a mansion that is typical of the masters' residences built last century. It makes an outstanding contribution to the history of modern art. Named after designer Georges Wakhevicht who lived in Tosny, the museum contains one hundred and fifty models of sets designed by him for the cinema, opera, and theatre. It also contains memorabilia connected with the artist.

The porch in Notre-Dame Church, Louviers.

CHÂTEAU-GAILLARD, A LOST DREAM!

In Igoville, visitors find themselves on the industrial right bank of the Seine. The tour of the *département* of Eure continues upstream.

Two meanders further on is Les Andelys, a major stopover on any tour of Normandy. Only the pages of a history book or the vagaries of the imagination can rebuild the fortress (Château-Gaillard) erected here in 1196 in a single year on the orders of Richard the Lionheart in order to prevent Philip Augustus of France from approaching the English sovereign's possessions. Only they can give an idea of the daring of the King of France's soldiers when they launched an attack against the fortress on 6th March 1204 by climbing in through the latrines and, once inside the castle that they had been besieging for five months, slaughtered its one hundred and eighty defenders and their leader, Roger de Lasci. Richard had died in Châlus five years earlier and was no longer there to defend the "one-year-old daughter" that he considered "so beautiful". John Lackland, who was rather more King of England than Duke of Normandy, showed little interest in the fate of the fortress, or in that of Rouen a few months later.

The barbican, the windowless lookout that protected the castle from attacks from the plain, the double line of fortifications built on the top of the sheer cliff overlooking the valley or moat, the keep in the centre, and the governor's apartments are no more than a few stretches of wall whose bonding is slowly being eaten away by the passing years. Henri IV and, later, Richelieu ordered the demolition of Château-Gaillard. Now it is little

Notre-Dame Church in Les Andelys.

more than a place steeped in nostalgia and memories of the Norman epic. It is also haunted by the ghost of Margaret of Burgundy whom Louis X, her husband, had strangled here and by memories of Blanche de la Marche who left the castle only to be shut away in a convent.

Château-Gaillard provides an unrivalled view of the Seine and Les Andelys. Jutting up from the houses and the thickets lining the river bank is the dome of the St. James Hospice (*hospice Saint-Jacques*), St. Saviour's Church (*église Saint-Sauveur*) and its spire and the more impressive steeple of Notre-Dame Church. Go back down into the town and push open the door in the porch of Notre-Dame,

a church built over a period of three hundred years between the 13th and 16th Centuries. The organ loft, statue of the Entombment of Christ, and stained-glass windows are the finest of its decorative features. The church also contains two paintings by Quentin Varin, teacher to that giant of the art world, Nicolas Poussin, who was born in 1594 in Villers near Les Andelys. A small museum nearby serves to keep alive his memory.

Visitors usually throw a coin into St. Clotilda's Fountain but without any hope of repeating the miracle that she worked there when she changed the water into wine for the workmen who, in the 6th Century, built Grand Andely Monastery.

GAILLON, "SIC TRANSIT..."

On the other bank of the river, some 12 kilometres (7 miles) away, is Gaillon! After being used as a prison then as barracks, the archbishop's palace built in 1490 for Georges I of Amboise, Archbishop of Rouen, is now a dilapidated castle. Its most outstanding, and the best-preserved, section is the gatehouse set in a solidly-enclosed courtyard, with two turrets and an axe-shaped roof. The gardens laid out by Le Nôtre have also disappeared.

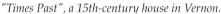

"Times Past", a 15th-century house in Vernon.

VERNON, THE SHARP TASTE OF CRESS

In the days when Normans and Frenchmen were at war, the tide flowed this far upstream. A convenient place, then, to set a country's border! This was the role of Vernon and it has retained a number of buildings to prove it. On the right bank are the towers and keep of Les Tourelles Castle, still standing guard over a few piles of the Old Bridge bristling with a half-timbered construction on the top. On the left bank is the Archives Tower built for Henry Beauclerc, where the stones still seem to resound to the echoing footsteps of soldiers in the service of the French king. In 1944, Vernon's geographical location caused it to be severely bombed.

The Seine from the ruins of Château-Gaillard in Les Andelys.

Bizy Castle.

The town is now steeped in an atmosphere of peace and tranquillity and is a constant source of delight for visitors. The Seine wends its bucolic way between the gardens on the left bank and the thickets on the right bank, past tiny islands dotted along its course like garlands of flowers. On June evenings, Vernon is filled with the scent of lime trees — there are 2,350 of them along its avenues and streets. The town's coat-of-arms (three bunches of cress tied with a golden thread) brings a sharp, fresh taste to the mouth. A few half-timbered houses (including the one called "Le Temps Jadis", literally "Times Past") are proof that the town enjoyed a certain degree of prosperity in days gone by.

In the Vernon Forest, on the right bank of the Seine, the S.E.P. produces

The Seahorses,
the famous statues in the park in Bizy.

the engines for the Ariane rocket. On the left bank, on the edge of the Bizy Forest, the castle of the same name has had an eventful history. It was partially razed to the ground during the French Revolution and was rebuilt for the first time for Louis-Philippe as a country house. Later, it was again rebuilt by Baron Schickler. It was he who commissioned the luxurious palace covered with a terrace of a lightness that contrasts with the splendour of the surviving 18th-century buildings. The furniture and imperial memorabilia filling its drawing rooms are, like its park (one might say, especially its park in which Charles Louis Fouquet had 76,000 trees planted and some admirable Baroque-style fountains installed), well worth a visit.

The mediaeval fortress in Gisors.

GISORS,
UNDERMINED
BY MYTHS

The enormous, dark fortress overlooking Gisors 30 kilometres (19 miles) to the north of Vernon has given the main town in the Norman Vexin area a reputation for strength.

From the 11th Century onwards, William Rufus, Henry Beauclerc, Henry II Plantagenet, Philip Augustus and Charles VII all commissioned work on this castle which is obviously impregnable with its outer wall supported by twelve towers and, in the centre, its awesome keep and tower. Sully decided to have it demolished but the castle escaped its fate and, once it had

become a listed building, underwent restoration in the first half of last century. Gisors is, therefore, one of the few mediaeval fortresses to have survived to the present day intact.

A catastrophe almost befell it, though. One night, in 1966, the St. Thomas Tower split open and it was realised that it had been undermined by archaeological digs undertaken by anonymous, but determined, treasure-seekers. A book stating that the Knights Templars' treasure was buried in the castle's underground passageways had whetted their appetite. It is true that the Knights

Volti: The Three Graces.

Vascœuil where Michelet once stayed, now a modern art centre.

Templar played an important role in Normandy and that they were, at one time, the guardians of Gisors but that was from 1158 to 1161, a long time before Philip the Fair sent them to the stake and, consequently, before they thought of burying their treasure trove.

The Norman Vexin area, of which Gisors is the main town, lies opposite the French Vexin. It is bordered by the R. Epte to the east and R. Andelle to the west.

The Andelle is a picturesque river that has inspired poets and caused many a romantic heart to

Fontaine-Guérard Abbey and the Andelle.

The covered market in Lyons-la-Forêt.

cult to distinguish from the walls of the abbey itself.

The castle in Vascoeuil Forest, which is admirable for its superb red brick dovecote, was the favourite residence of historian Jules Michelet. His study has been reconstructed in the tower beside the castle and a collection of memorabilia has been put on display in a small museum.

North of the Vexin area is the Lyons Forest, State-owned woodland covering 11,000 hectares within both Eure and Seine-Maritime. Lyons-la-Forêt on the banks of the R. Lieure is an archetypal Norman village with half-timbered houses, 18th-century covered market, and church with ashlar and flint bonding.

Mortemer Abbey was demolished during the French Revolution in order to provide building stone for the village of Lisors. The remaining stonework provides a gran-

beat faster. Pîtres, where the river flows into the Seine, is the setting for the legend of the Coast of the Two Lovers, a major theme in French literature. Fontaine-Guérard Abbey on the banks of the river is a very romantic set of ruins. Founded in 1185, only the chapel dedicated to St. Michael, the chevet of the minster, the chapter house and the nuns' dorter have survived. The stones were used to built a Neo-Gothic threadmill not far away. The factory burned down and all that remains of it are a few stretches of ivy-clad wall that, in some places, are diffi-

The ruins of the Cistercian abbey in Mortemer.

diose testimony to religious architecture in the 12th and 13th Centuries.

Beyond the forest, in the direction of Les Andelys, the Collegiate Church of Notre-Dame d'Ecouis is considered to have the richest collection of statues in Normandy. An Ecce Homo, a recumbent statue of Jean Enguerrand de Marigny and a Mary Magdalen with long, wavy hair flowing down over her entire body are just some of the finest pieces.

Water lilies in Claude Monet's garden.

St. John the Baptist, a statue in the collegiate church in Ecouis.

GIVERNY, IMPRESSIONISM AT ITS PEAK

In 1883, Claude Monet rented a building and barn in Giverny and turned them into his home and studio. The very modest village stretching along the right-hand hillside of the Epte Valley was about to become universally famous.

The world-wide popularity of the Impressionist School, of which Monet was the father, has made Giverny one of the most cherished tourist attractions in Normandy. From spring to the first cold days of winter, more than 400,000 visitors enter the artist's house and invade the garden beyond its long façade divided by its balcony-promenade and brightened by its pink pebbledash, green shutters, ivy geraniums and rose trees.

The property was bequeathed to the Academy of Fine Arts by Claude Monet's second son in 1966 and was reconstructed as it had been in the artist's lifetime by the Claude-Monet Foundation and the curator Gérald Van der Kamp. The drawing room, bedrooms and kitchen have been repainted in the same colours as they were when the artist lived here. His Japanese engravings have been put back on the walls. Some of the flowers in

Claude Monet's house and garden.

the garden are common; others are very rare. All of them are of the species planted by Monet. The pond in the water garden, which was created by diverting an arm of the R. Epte, has been cleaned and the famous water lilies now bloom again beneath the Japanese bridge.

Visitors make a pilgrimage to the very source of the artist's inspiration, almost violating his everyday privacy. Most of them ignore his tomb in the nearby cemetery where he has lain since 1926.

Near the house is a white stone construction trying to push its way out of a garden that is just asking to grow. This is the twin of the Terra Museum of Chicago. Founded by Daniel Terra and his wife, its aim is to make the public more aware of American painters who were inspired by France. They came over in large numbers during the Impressionist period and were frequent visitors to Giverny where, apparently, Monet usually ignored them although Lilla Cabot Perrit, who had arrived in the village before him, gave him a great deal of advice when he was designing his garden. Because Giverny's destiny is so closely linked to painting, a few artists have settled here today. The Hôtel Baudy, where the Impressionists used to stay, is now the town's third museum and art gallery.

Seine-Maritime, the cradle of Normandy

Seine-Maritime is the largest of the *départements* in Normandy and the most densely-populated with 1,220,000 people, most of whom live in towns. Its economy is based on the sea, the land and industry. Le Havre and Rouen, its largest cities, are among the leading ports in France. One-third of the country's oil-refining capacity centres on this area. The Bray and Caux areas, however, are lush farming regions and the Brotonne, Roumarc, La Londe and Eawy Forests cover more than 50,000 hectares.

Normandy was born in Seine-Maritime on the banks of the R. Epte, one hundred years after the first Viking invasions in Seine Bay. Its heritage is as vast as its geographical area; it contains 188 historic monuments and 347 listed buildings.

The Seine at Grand-Couronne.

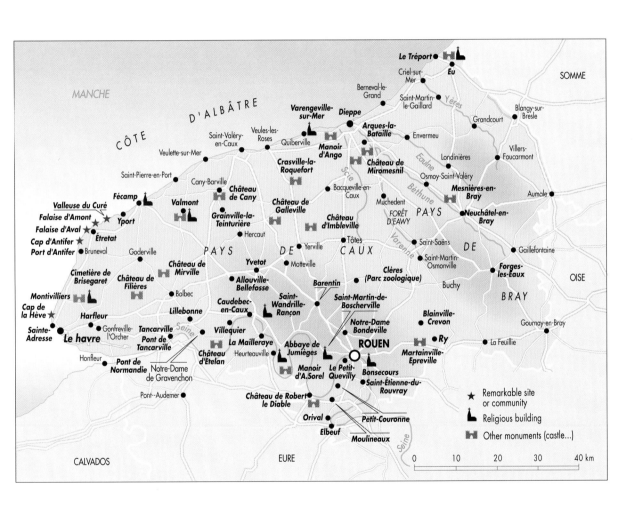

MANCHE

CÔTE D'ALBÂTRE

SOMME

Le Tréport
Criel-sur-Mer
Eu
Berneval-le-Grand
Saint-Martin-le-Gaillard
Grandcourt
Blangy-sur-Bresle

Varengeville-sur-Mer
Dieppe
Saint-Valéry-en-Caux
Veules-les-Roses
Quiberville
Manoir d'Ango
Arques-la-Bataille
Envermeu
Londinières
Villers-Foucarmont

Veulette-sur-Mer
Saint-Pierre-en-Port
Cany-Barville
Crasville-la-Roquefort
Château de Miromesnil
Bacqueville-en-Caux
Osmoy-Saint-Valéry

Scie
Béthune

Fécamp
Château de Cany
Château de Galleville
Muchedent
FORÊT D'EAWY
PAYS
Mesnières-en-Bray
Aumale

Valleuse du Curé
Valmont
Grainville-la-Teinturière
Château d'Imbleville
Neuchâtel-en-Bray

Falaise d'Amont
Yport
Hercaut
Yerville
Tôtes
Varenne

Falaise d'Aval
Étretat
Motteville
Saint-Saëns
Gaillefontaine

Cap d'Antifer
Port d'Antifer
Bruneval
Goderville
PAYS
DE
CAUX
Saint-Martin-Osmonville

Cimetière de Brisegaret
Château de Mirville
Yvetot
Clères (Parc zoologique)
Buchy
Forges-les-Eaux

Château de Filières
Allouville-Bellefosse
Barentin
Saint-Martin-de-Boscherville
DE
BRAY
OISE

Montivilliers
Bolbec
Blainville-Crevon

Cap de la Hève
Harfleur
Lillebonne
Caudebec-en-Caux
Saint-Wandrille-Rançon
Notre-Dame Bondeville
Ry
Gournay-en-Bray

Sainte-Adresse
Le havre
Gonfreville-l'Orcher
Villequier
La Mailleraye
ROUEN
Martainville-Epreville
La Feuillie

Tancarville
Pont de Tancarville
Château d'Etelan
Heurteauville
Abbaye de Jumièges
Bonsecours

Honfleur
Pont de Normandie
Notre-Dame de Gravenchon
Manoir d'A.Sorel
Le Petit-Quevilly
Saint-Étienne-du-Rouvray

Pont-Audemer
Château de Robert le Diable
Petit-Couronne

Orival
Elbeuf
Moulineaux

Seine

★ Remarkable site or community

Religious building

Other monuments (castle...)

0   10   20   30   40 km

CALVADOS

EURE

A tour of Normandy

LE HAVRE, THE EYES OF THE PRESENT

This is the largest city in the province as far as its population is concerned (200,000) and Le-Havre-de-Grâce is the antithesis of everybody's idea of a typical Norman town with half-timbered houses huddling round a Romanesque or Gothic church. Because of this, it is ignored by a large number of guidebooks and excluded from sightseeing tours. Yet this is quite wrong. This city should be seen with the eyes of the present and not through a haze of nostalgia.

Graville Abbey, far from the city centre, is the oldest reminder of times past. Le Havre is a modern town, created in 1517 by François I in an effort to give his kingdom a major port. But the deluge of iron and fire that rained down on it in September 1944 left few traces of the first few centuries of prosperity except for the 16th and 17th-century cathedral, old houses such as the Bocage de Bleville Residence which is now the Old Havre Museum, or the former law courts that now house the Natural History Museum, all of them restored.

The architect and town planner, Auguste Perret, who was put in charge of the town's reconstruction, retained the checkerboard layout used by Bellarmoto, the first designer of Le Havre, but left open many of the areas that had been flattened by the war. He was a passionate believer in the value of reinforced concrete and used it almost to the exclusion of any other material in the rebuilding of the town. His choice has given Le Havre a reputation for being a cold city lacking in humanity but this is an opinion that must now be reconsidered.

The Town Hall square.

The harbour. Originally called Havre de Grâce, it gave a shortened version of its name to the town, Le Havre.

St. Joseph's Church.

Gardens, ponds and fountains fill and enliven the square in front of the Town Hall. This is one of the largest squares in Europe (243 metres by 192 metres - 263 yds by 208 yds) but it made people feel so small that they tended to scurry across it to get to the other side. Avenue Foch is as wide as the Champs-Elysées in Paris, a superb, majestic avenue with pedestrian areas where people can enjoy a stroll. It leads from the Town Hall to the Porte Océane, the beautiful name given to Le Havre and embodied in the space between two tall tower blocks overlooking the sea.

Le Havre is a city of longitudinal views. The footbridge crossing the Commerce Basin provides one of the finest. Beyond the war memorial are the twin buildings of the Oscar Niemeyer Arts Centre, named after the Brazilian architect who designed it and, by doing so, introduced a few curves into an environment where straight lines reigned supreme. Further away, like a gigantic lighthouse, there is the bell-tower of St. Joseph's Church rising to a height of 110 metres (358 ft.) above the terraces on the apartment blocks below. This church is built entirely of concrete and can only be appreciated at its full architectural value from the inside.

The Espace Oscar-Niemeyer.

Notre-Dame, the cathedral with the unexpected architecture.

A tour of Normandy

"This was a marvellous spot. The view extended across the entire town" (André Siegfried).

Modern architects have also used their talents to serve the world of painting, a major art form in Le Havre where Eugène Boudin and Monet, his pupil, invented Impressionism and where Dufy, Friesz and Dubuffet were all born. On the seafront, seen through The Eye, is the Malraux Museum built of glass, aluminium, and steel, one of the most remarkable museums in France. Le Havre has Normandy's third university and it has given a number of great names to literature, sociology, music and politics among them Bernardin de Saint-Pierre, Casimir Delavigne, Raymond Queneau, Armand Salacrou, André Siegfried, Arthur Honegger, and René Coty.

It is, though, the "ever-present" sea that keeps people in Le Havre.

Not to mention the harbour — 20,000 hectares of basins, 28 kilometres (17 miles) of wharves and quaysides, and the François I lock which is one of the largest in the world (400 metres (433 yds.) long and 67 metres (73 yds.) wide). The port of Le Havre, whose history and craftsmen are the subject of a museum, is now the second largest commercial harbour in France after Marseilles and the fifth largest in Europe. Fifty million tonnes of goods pass through it every year and Antifer, its extension, can cater for the largest tankers in the world.

Eight thousand hectares of industrial estate line the Grand Canal du Havre and the Canal de Tancarville, beneath the 240-metre (780-foot) chimneys of the power station. Oil refineries (Gonfreville,

Port-Jérôme, Notre-Dame-de-Gravenchon), petro-chemical plants and mechanical engineering companies (Renault in Sandouville) make this a major industrial centre.

To the west of the city, St. Adresse Fort near the chapel of Our Lady of the Waves (Notre-Dame-des-Flots) and the "Sugar Loaf", the headland of La Hève, and a few streets in the upper town provide a panoramic view of the city, its harbour, its suburbs and the estuary. The town of Sainte-Adresse set beneath the cliff face is an extension of the city itself and is its residential district and seaside resort, sometimes nicknamed "the Nice of Le Havre". The Dufaye Palace is the most famous of its houses. During the 1914-1918 war, it accommodated the Belgian government.

Seine-Maritime, the cradle of Normandy

Harfleur: a bell-tower 93 metres - 302 ft. high.

Montgeon Forest and Les Rouelles Park with its arboretum and 17th and 18th-century farm are not far from the city and they provide plenty of opportunity for relaxation. In Gonfreville-l'Orcher, an old feudal fortress was replaced by a Louis XV residence with a superb park and dovecote. The narrow streets and old houses of Montivillers have grown up around the abbey founded by St. Philibert and the church, topped by a fine Romanesque tower, includes two naves built at an interval of five hundred years. The Brisegaret Cemetery in the same parish is a small version of the Saint-Maclou graveyard. And finally, Harfleur has the tallest and most beautiful bell-tower in the Caux area and owes some of its fame to Victor Hugo who wrote, "Nor the sails in the distance going down to Harfleur".

THE SEINE VALLEY - CARGO SHIPS BETWEEN ABBEYS AND CHERRY TREES

As the crow flies, less than 80 kilometres (50 miles) separate Le Havre and Rouen but, to go from one to the other, the R. Seine covers a distance of more than 120 kilometres (75 miles) changing direction from one meander to the next.

The Seine is no longer the river painted by Sisley, described by Maupassant or Maurois or inspiring Frédéric Bérat to write the verses and refrain of his song, "J'irai voir ma Normandie" ("I'll go and see my Normandy"). Hugo and Lamartine, both of whom were members of parliament, demanded that its banks be developed and their demands were met.

Tancarville, the oldest of the bridges over the lower reaches of the Seine.

TANCARVILLE, VILLEQUIER, CAUDEBEC - SMILES AND TRAGEDY

Still, the Seine Valley remains a huge book with pages depicting the architectural and natural heritage, a book that people like to "read", forgetting the pages that have been rather too dog-eared by the industrial activities of man.

Tancarville is the name of a bridge, but for many more years it was the name of a cliff, an unrivalled lookout post at the mouth of the Seine. A fortress was built here in the Middle Ages and a few traces of it can still be seen. They blend into the walls of the castle built in the 18th Century for Louis de La Tour d'Auvergne. A few miles away is Etelan Castle, built

A bust of Victor Hugo's daughter, Léopoldine.

The Victor-Hugo Museum in Villequier.

Seine-Maritime, the cradle of Normandy

Statuettes on the doorway of the church in Caudebec-en-Caux.

three hundred years earlier in the Flamboyant Gothic style and, again, designed as a country house rather than as a fortress. The stained-glass windows, statues and paintings in its chapel are outstandingly beautiful.

For anybody touring the meanders of the Seine, Villequier is a literary stop-over steeped in tragedy. It was here, on 4th September 1843, that Charles Vacquerie and his young wife, Léopoldine, were swept away by the tidal bore. She was the daughter of Victor Hugo and the poet immortalised her in his work, turning a personal drama into a catastrophe that touched everybody. Everybody knows the lines:
Et quand j'arriverai, je mettrai sur sa tombe
Un bouquet de verdure et de bruyère en fleurs.
(And when I arrive, I shall place on her grave
A bouquet of greenery and heather in bloom.)

A stop in Caudebec between the Sainte-Gertrude Valley and the Rançon Valley is a happier experience. Although the town still provides much for the nostalgics, visitors can also enjoy a stroll in the gardens along the banks of the Seine, see the Knights Templars' house, tour the museum describing the town's rich maritime history, and, most of all, step into its church, a pure gem of Flamboyant Gothic architecture described by Henri IV as "the most beautiful chapel in all the kingdom". Its portal is decorated with a host of statues, a working-class procession of stonemasons and stone-cutters who gave later generations their own portraits and those of their fellow workers by carving them in limestone. Guillaume Le Tellier, the architect, included one engineering feat in his design — the enormous hanging keystone in the Lady Chapel immediately above his tomb.

SAINT-WANDRILLE,
A LIVING MONASTERY

There is not a tower or pinnacle to guide visitors from Caudebec to Saint-Wandrille set in the depths of the Fontenelle Valley that gave the abbey its original name. History has demolished its most outstanding buildings but it has never really succeeded in totally destroying the abbey.

In 858 A.D, the Vikings set fire to the first monastery founded two hundred years earlier by Wandrille, a dignitary at the court of King Dagobert. One thousand years later, the French Revolution scattered its monks - and its stones. Sold off as national property, it was turned into a threadmill then, later, into a source of building stone. The 12th and 13th-century minster soon consisted of no more than a few pillars, one wall of the transept, and a few bases of columns overgrown with grass. The cloister galleries remained intact but the sculptures that used to decorate them, like the ones on the doors into the refectory and on the lavabo, were damaged.

Saint-Wandrille, though, does not attract visitors for its ruins. The abbey became a religious community again in 1931. The Maurists who had already saved it from total ruin came back to the remaining abbey buildings. They spend their life, between services sung in plainchant, in study and in the work needed to enable the community to subsist. They also welcome visitors in search of the history of the monastery or spiritual guidance.

Saint-Wandrille, the abbey that is still very much alive.

JUMIÈGES,
ADMIRABLE RUINS

They have given the abbey back its church by dismantling then reassembling the tithe barn from La Neuville-du-Bosc in Eure and turning it into their new chapel. St. Wandrille's head, contained in a contemporary reliquary, has been placed in the church that has marked the re-establishment of a religious community first founded one thousand three hundred years ago and still alive today.

In the capital "O" of one of the meanders of the Seine stands Jumièges Abbey, its two decapitated towers outlined on the horizon and flanking a gable with no roof. This is still one of the main images of the region, a picture that remains in the mind's eye.

Fontenelle and Jumièges are less than two leagues apart and their destiny was similar. Indeed, it did not diverge until recent times. There is no religious community in Jumièges. Where could they live anyway? As

historian R. de Lasteyrie puts it, the abbey is nothing more than "one of the most admirable ruins in France".

Notre-Dame was once one of the finest Romanesque churches ever built in Normandy; now all that remain are the two towers 43 metres (140 ft.) high flanking the west front, the three-storeyed walls of the nave and the west wall of the lantern-tower, a gem of harmony and balance. The remainder of the lantern-tower was blown up with dynamite so that the demolition work would be completed more quickly. St. Peter's (*église Saint-Pierre*), Saint-Wandrille's "twin", was built in the 10th Century then reconstructed in the 13th in the Gothic style but it has not been spared. Only the site of the cloisters can be seen. The undercroft and chapter house had already lost their roof by the time the picks and pickaxes were stilled in 1824. Only the 14th-century gatehouse, the abbot's lodgings (a fine 17th-century construction in the middle of lawns), and the monumental staircase linking the two levels in the park were left standing.

The apartments have been turned into a museum containing, most notably, the famous recumbent statue of the "Unnerved of Jumièges" about which so much has been written and said and the tombstone of Agnès Sorel. The "Lady of Beauty", Charles VII's mistress, died nearby at Les Vignes Manor. She was buried beneath the pavement of St. Peter's.

Jumièges, "one of the most admirable sets of ruins...".

SAINT-GEORGES-DE-BOSCHERVILLE, PAST AND PRESENT UNITED

Saint-Georges-de-Boscherville, the third of the abbeys in the Seine Valley, had a happier fate when, in 1791, it became the parish church of Saint-Martin-de-Boscherville.

Its main characteristics are its unity, austerity and harmony. In the 13th Century, ogival vaulting replaced the original timber rafters. Friezes underscore the arches and there are a few low reliefs with an archaic form of decoration; these are its only ornamentation. The abbey buildings dating from the 17th Century beyond the transept do not interrupt the overall sense of balance. Indeed, they leave the church its original spirituality. Like its setting. There are no parks, gardens, or huge trees here; just the countryside of Normandy with the Roumare Forest in the background.

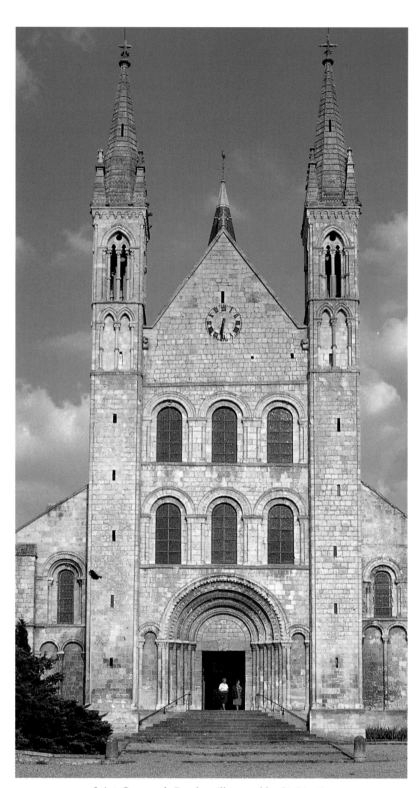

Saint-Georges de Boscherville, saved by St. Martin.

Seine-Maritime, the cradle of Normandy

THE LEFT BANK AND
THE THIRD ESTATE

A partly-ruined tower topped by a flapping red standard decorated with the two gold leopards of Normandy rises high above the hillsides cloaked in the La Londe Forest with the towns of Moulineaux and La Bouille at their foot. This is the castle of Robert the Devil, a mythical figure created by the troubadours of the Middle Ages and the popular novels of the 19th Century, said by some to be none other than Robert the Magnificent, the father of William the Conqueror. Built in the 11th Century for the Dukes of Normandy and demolished in the 15th Century, the ruined fortress now contains a museum in which the waxworks try to recreate the Viking epic.

La Bouille is an attractive, sleepy little town still redolent of literary greatness and the heyday of river barges. Almost in its centre is a bourgeois house which was the birthplace of Hector Malot, the very popular author of *Sans Famille, En Famille* and some seventy other novels.

Beyond Yville Castle, a tour of the Seine Valley goes from orchard to thicket and from farmstead to cottage. There are few manor houses or abbeys here. It is as if the nobility and clergy had shunned this bank, leaving it for the Third Estate of craftsmen and peasants. From Herteauville to Duclair, the road is known as the Fruit Trail. From La Mailleraye to Saint-Samson de la Roques, it is the Cottage Trail. Both routes skirt the 7,000-hectare Brotonne Forest which shares its name with the "Regional Country Park" set up in 1974 to ensure the protection of the natural environment and enhance the area's heritage.

The castle that once belonged to the mythical Robert the Devil.

A tour of Normandy

ETRETAT, SLASHED BY THE SEA AND THE WIND

From the Seine Estuary to the mouth of the R. Bresle, the Caux area drops straight down into the sea. The coastline is, in some places such as Cap Fragnet, more than 100 metres (325 ft.) high; over a distance of 130 kilometres (81 miles), it is an unbroken line of chalk cliffs striated with thin layers of flint.

Of all its beauty spots, Etretat is the most famous. Yet nothing here is manmade. Only the sea and the wind have cut into the fragile limestone to create this needle 80 metres (260 ft.) high and the arches resting against the cliffs, with a vault at La Manneporte that rises to a height of 100 metres (325 ft.) above the seaweed-clad rocks at low tide.

Huddling behind the dyke that protects it when the sea is running strong and clashing against the famous pebbles, the village is now a small town of restaurants and "Edwardian" villas swimming in a sea of pink and blue hydrangeas. A steep footpath leads up to the top of the Aval Cliff from which the view extends beyond La Manneporte to Antifer. Eastwards, there is a road to the Falaise d'Amont — and a superb panoramic view stretching beyond Yport.

The Alabaster Coast, thus named because of the colour of the water as it dissolves the limestone, unfurls a seemingly endless line of beauty spots such as Valleuse du Curé or the Belval Needle. Some places, though, have been given up in the interests of the local economy e.g. the harbour at Antifer, or the nuclear power stations in Paluel and Penly.

FÉCAMP, WHERE EVEN CRAFTS ARE LEGENDARY

A monastery founded to house a relic of the Precious Blood but destroyed by the Vikings and rebuilt by William Longsword eventually developed into Fécamp. The Church of the Holy and Indivisible Trinity (_église de la Sainte-et-Indivisible Trinité_) built over the ruins of the original monastery is one of the finest and largest in France.

Near the port, the Neo-Gothic and Neo-Renaissance buildings of "La Bénédictine" are another, physical, example of Fécamp's fame. They are among the most popular places to visit in Normandy, attracting 130,000 people every year. A few of the rooms contain displays relating to the history of the famous liqueur invented in 1510 by a monk called Bernardo Vincelli, using plants that grew in the valley

Fécamp: the harbour and Benedictine monastery.

"The wall that we have on the sea..." (Victor Hugo, Les Travailleurs de la mer).

A tour of Normandy

The nave in the Church of the Holy Trinity.

The Still Room in the Bénédictine Liqueur Museum.

The Tabernacle of the Precious Blood.

around Fécamp. It was not manufactured and marketed by a person from Fécamp, however, until 1863. He was Alexandre Le Grand and the liqueur made his fortune. The laboratory and cellars where the elixir is left to mature are still in the same building but the distillery is now elsewhere. The premises also house a museum of objets d'art and books from the abbey. An 18th-century mansion contains the Arts Centre museum in which arguably the most unusual collection is the one of baby bottles. Some of them date from Antiquity.

In this town steeped in legend, the harbour at the foot of the cliffs topped by the chapel of Our Lady of Salvation (*Notre-Dame-du-Salut*) has been the cradle of a legendary craft, that of the Newfoundland fisherman. The epic tale of these men can be relived in the museum.

"Dieppe,... a very luminous town with clean streets" (Chateaubriand, Memories from Beyond the Tomb).

DIEPPE,
A PLACE TO DREAM
OF "NEW STARS"

Dieppe has played a leading but often little-known role in history. It was bombed in 1694 by the Anglo-Dutch fleet and totally flattened. It was never to regain the sparkle that had been its main characteristic during the Renaissance period.

Although this is the fourth largest town in Seine-Maritime and is a sub-prefecture, it has a population of only 40,000. Yet it is a busy place with an impressive group of historic buildings and is a pleasant place to stop for a while after seeing it from the heights of Le

A tour of Normandy

Dieppe Castle, the residence of the Governors.

An ivory in the museum.

Pollet or from the platform at the castle.

It was from Dieppe Harbour, where one million passengers from England disembark every year, that Jean de Bethencourt, Jean Cousin, Raoul and Jean Parmentier, Verrazano, and Champlain set sail. The links with Canada were further strengthened in 1942 when 6,000 soldiers from that country died or were taken prisoner after landing on the local beaches on 19th August. Numerous maple leaf emblems and a memorial on Square du Canada keep alive the memory of the connections and the sacrifice.

The sea has pride of place in Dieppe where there are five museums dealing with some particular aspect of the subject. The beach here was the first seaside resort in France when the Duchess de Berry launched the fashion for sea bathing in 1823. Numerous artists have also set up their easels on the shore, among them Pissaro, Monet, Renoir, Sisley, Dufy and Braque, to name but a few.

Of course, they also set up their easels at the corners of the old streets of white brick houses on which the vividly-coloured frontages support wrought-iron balconies. And on the bustling quaysides in the harbour where they could watch the fishing fleet, foot passengers, commercial vessels and yachts. Or in front of the chevet of St. James' Church (*église Saint-Jacques*) which is "as large as a cathedral". Over the centuries, shipowners and seafarers have embellished it with votive offerings. In the Treasure Chapel, a carved frieze represents the "savages" they met during their expeditions.

The towers and ramparts of the castle stand high above the town. Built on the remains of an older

Miromesnil where Maupassant was born.

The dovecot in the manor that once belonged to Jean Ango.

fortress, it now houses a museum with an entire section devoted to ivory carvings because, for four centuries, Dieppe was the ivory capital.

Varangeville nearby was the home of the famous shipowner Jean Ango. The castle and dovecote are admirable pieces of building work. On the cliff is a 13th-century church in the middle of a sailors' cemetery. Among the graves are those of dramatist Porto-Riche, composer Albert Roussel and artist Georges Braque.

Upstream in the Arques Valley is an impressive set of fortifications overlooking Arques-la-Bataille and its 16th-century church. The Count of Arques, Henry Beauclerc, and François I all had a hand in its building or its extension until it was destroyed during the French Revolution. The history lesson is perhaps more interesting than the lesson in military architecture demanded by the square keep and the towers that seem to defy all sense of balance. Eléonore of Brittany and Joan of Arc were the most famous prisoners to have been kept in its dungeons.

Lost at the end of a road so tiny it is little more than a path is Miromesnil Castle, the birthplace on 5th August 1850 of the great novelist Guy de Maupassant.

A tour of Normandy

LE TRÉPORT AND EU,
THE ORDINARY PEOPLE AND
THE ARISTOCRACY

A general view of Tréport.

The suburbs of Tréport, the working-class town, and Eu, the aristocratic community, lie on the Bresle Estuary, seemingly flirting with each other.

A road, a long pedestrian walkway and a cable car all lead from the town of Tréport up to the observation platform at Les Terrasses. From a spot near the Sailors' Cross, there is a superb view of the Picardy coast (or Opal Coast) and Le Tréport.

Built between the quaysides of a harbour that is always full of colourful bustle, Le Tréport is both a seaside resort with a long beach of fine sand (this is the nearest beach to Paris) and a small town which is lively whatever the season. Its church and the Musoir Cross on the market square are its main sights.

A few miles upstream lies Eu, barring the horizon in the valley with the frontage of its castle which is more than 90 metres (293 ft.) long. It was Mademoiselle de Montpensier who extended the castle built originally by Henri of Guise and, later, it was Louis-Philippe's favourite residence. The Count and Countess of Paris were its last occupants and it was they who added to the gardens designed by Le Nôtre the colours of the rhododendrons and azaleas planted there in large numbers. The castle is now the Town Hall. It also contains a museum with memorabilia relating to Louis-Philippe and an extensive display concerning the glass-making industry of which the Bresle Valley used to be a major centre.

Thanks to the de Guise family, Eu was probably one of the first towns in France to have a secondary school. Set up in 1588, the austere

Eu Castle, Louis-Philippe's favourite place of residence.

walls of the establishment can be seen in the town centre. It is now the Anguier High School, named after two great 17th-century sculptors who were pupils here. In the chancel of the chapel are two magnificent white marble mausoleums, the tombs of Henri de Guise who succumbed to the blows of Henri III's hired assassins and his wife, Catherine, an inconsolable widow who commissioned the two pieces of sculpture.

The collegiate church in Eu, near the high school, is the town's pride and joy. Its well-balanced architecture, stained-glass windows, pulpit, organ loft, and statues are just some of the features that give it its beauty. Its crypt contains the recumbent statues of the d'Artois family. These tombs were not desecrated and scattered during the French Revolution.

THE BRAY AREA - IRON, WATER AND CHEESE

The Bray area gives visitors a chance to enjoy a breath of fresh air and some rural scenery in a tour that otherwise tends to take in a large number of historic monuments and listed buildings.

Forges-les-Eaux, one of the larger towns in the area, reflects its history in its name. It was a metal-working community before becoming a spa town. Discovered in 1573 by the Governor of Gisors, the medicinal properties of its mineral water attracted the attention of Louis XIII, Anne of Austria and Richelieu, among others. Three of the five springs were therefore called the "Royale", the "Reinette" ("little queen") and the "Cardinale". Its lush vegetation, lakes and wide tree-lined avenues including the one leading to a former friary that preceded the casino, added to a few buildings on the periphery that are representative of the "spa town style", go together to give Forges its charm.

A cheese, Neufchâtel, brought fame to the town of the same name but it was a farmer's wife from Gournay who brought prosperity to the area by inventing the "petit suisse", a blend of curds and cream. The Bray area produces more fromage frais than any other area in France.

Not far from Neufchâtel is Mesnières Castle, one of the most outstanding Renaissance buildings in Normandy.

The charms of Forges-les-Eaux.

A tour of Normandy

THE CAUX AREA, UNCHANGING SCENERY!

The Caux area was made famous by Maupassant and a few others. The tales he told of this region are no longer up to date but the scenery and landscape has changed very little since that time.

Yvetot took the title of "Capital of the Caux Area" from Caudebec and it now has the Caux area folk museum. Béranger, who poked fun at the "little king of Yvetot" was no doubt unaware that the kings of France themselves used this title for the local lord. The modern church in Yvetot, which was built in 1956 in the shape of a rotunda, shows great originality in its design. The stained-glass windows were all by Max Ingrand and were the great master glass-painter's finest masterpiece.

Near Yvetot, on the side of the RD 94 road is the Allouville Oak, one of the unusual sights in Normandy. The tree is several hundred years old and was planted at the entrance to the graveyard and church. Every spring, its main branches and shoots still turn green. However, it is not so much famous for its age as for the chapel built in its trunk in 1696 by the local parish priest.

A statue of the Virgin Mary in Valmont.

VALMONT, THE FORGOTTEN TOWN

Manor houses and castles are no less numerous here than in the other areas of Normandy and those that are worth a mention for their architecture, their surroundings or their links with history include Galleville, Imbleville, Crasville-le-Roquefort, Cany, Mirville and Filières whose sevenfold row of beech trees is nicknamed the "Cathedral".

Grainville-la-Teinturière is also worth a visit. This was the birthplace of Jean de Bethencourt who discovered the Canary Islands and became their king but was forced to sell them to the King of Castile before returning to his home village

The Allouville Oak.

A stained-glass window by Max Ingrand.

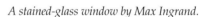

Valmont Castle, family home of the d'Estoutevilles.

where he died. The museum houses a collection of memorabilia.

Valmont at the other end of the plateau is the cradle of a great Norman family, the d'Estoutevilles. Robert II d'Estouteville had the castle built; his brother, Nicolas, commissioned the abbey of which only the chancel, transept and one apsidal chapel have survived. However, the ethereal architecture of the chapel, the decoration in its vaulted roof, its stained-glass windows and, more particularly, in the "small chamber", the group of statues representing the Annunciation of the Blessed Virgin Mary make a visit to Valmont extremely interesting from an artistic point of view.

On the way back to Le Havre, it is worth stopping in Mannéville

where the church is one of the finest buildings in Normandy. Near Rouen is Clères Zoo, founded in 1919 by Jean Delacour and still attracting large numbers of visitors. In superb natural surroundings, they can see kangaroos, antelopes, and gibbons in semi-liberty, as well as pink flamingos, tropical geese and ducks, and cranes. The aviaries are filled with pheasants, pigeons, budgerigars, and a whole host of tropical birds.

Lillebonne, a few miles away, is an introduction to Normandy — before you get there. Once the main town of the Caleti tribe, it was a major harbour on the Bolbec Estuary but the port has now silted up. Its amphitheatre, covered with vegetation, used to hold 10,000 spectators.

Pink flamingoes in the park in Clères.

A tour of Normandy

THE SUBURBS OF ROUEN - INDUSTRIAL HERITAGE

Where are the real boundaries of the suburbs of Rouen? Each official body seems to have its own, so that the population ranges from 400,000 to 700,000, or even more!

This is a highly-industrial area. A few companies or sectors of activity have made a name for the surrounding towns, as have abbeys or castles. Among them are the refinery at Petit-Couronne, fertiliser plant in Petit-Quevilly, papermill in Saint-Etienne du Rouvray, car plant in Cléon etc. Some of the buildings erected last century are now considered as an integral part of the area's heritage and are being restored rather than demolished.

One such is the factory built by Louis Fromage to produce the first elasticated fabrics; it now houses the Normandy College of Architecture (*école d'architecture de Normandie*). Another is the ropewalk in Notre-D... Bondeville. Then there a... mills on the rivers Ro... Aubette, or the Foudre factory... Petit-Quevilly.

The porch on the church in Ry, which features in Madame Bovary under the name of "Yonville l'Abbaye".

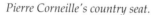

Pierre Corneille's country seat.

BARENTIN, A MUSEUM IN THE STREET

Barentin owes its nickname of "a museum in the street" to one of its mayors, André Marie, who was also a government minister during the Fourth Republic. He had almost three hundred statues erected in the streets of his town, some of them by such prestigious names as Rodin, Bourdelle, Janiot or Lebourgeois.

It was from Cantelou that Maupassant described the young industrial Rouen in his novel, *Bel Ami*. In Croisset, only a summer house remains in the gardens of the large family house where Flaubert spent much of his life.

Bonsecours to the east of Rouen, right at the top of the St. Catherine Hill, is a residential suburb and the

114

setting for a pilgrimage to Notre-Dame.

Beyond it, in the countryside, another "pilgrimage" takes people to Ry and Blainville-Crevon, in the footsteps of Delphine Couturier, the wife of a man named Delamare, whose unhappy fate was said to have provided Flaubert with the inspiration for his novel, Madame Bovary.

Martainville Castle only a short distance away is now the *département's* Museum of Norman Traditions and Arts.

Petit-Couronne was dramatist Pierre Corneille's country retreat.

ELBEUF, IN THE DAYS OF THE DRAPERS

Elbeuf, set at the confluence of the Oison and the Seine, is a large industrial town. Its main activity from the Middle Ages onwards was the production of cloth.

Although it has now replaced cloth-making by other industries, Elbeuf and its population of 60,000 still has something of a 19th-century working-class town about it. The church of St. Stephen and St. John (*Saint-Etienne and Saint-Jean*) bear witness to a more distant, more prosperous past. One of their stained-glass windows, dating from the 16th Century, depicts drapers at work.

On the Elbeuf to Oissel road, Seine-Maritime, which is decidedly very varied as regards landscapes and buildings, offers visitors a strange beauty spot — the Orival Rocks.

The Orival Rocks carved by the Seine.

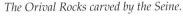

A tour of Normandy

ROUEN, A LIVELY MUSEUM-TOWN

Rouen is the capital of Normandy, the seat of the regional prefecture of Upper Normandy, and the "county town" of Seine-Maritime yet it has a population of scarcely 102,000, or 380,000 if the suburbs are included in the figures. The R. Seine has, like its history, divided it into two towns connected by five bridges.

On the left bank is the working-class town. The 80-metre (260-foot) Archives Tower, devoid of windows, was built in 1965 in the middle of the buildings constituting "county hall" across which it lays its long shadow. Its history goes back perhaps only two hundred years, very little compared to the two thousand year old history of Rouen, the former capital of the Veliocasses, and a major Gallo-Roman town in the Second Lyonnaise area. It used to be an industrial town described by Maupassant or Mac Orlan but the left bank is now given over to the tertiary sector and shops. For visitors with time on their hands, this is a prelude to, or an extension of, a tour of Rouen.

The right bank is the town of architectural and historical interest, with roofs that huddle together beneath the spires and towers of

Below: The remains of St. Saviour's discovered beneath Place du Vieux-Marché.

Seine-Maritime, the cradle of Normandy

Opposite: *Rouen's most famous sight, the Great Clock.*

"When the smoke cleared, it became apparent that Rouen would still have enough masterpieces" (in this instance

the Law Courts) "to provide glory and honour for one hundred towns" (André Maurois, Rouen dévasté).

A tour of Normandy

Notre-Dame, St. Ouen's Church, St. Maclou's etc. These are the "one hundred bell-towers" described by Victor Hugo. Rouen is a place to visit theme by theme although one tends to run into another. A church will send you in search of Joan of Arc. The law courts serve as a reminder of Corneille etc.

Let us begin with the churches, and the most outstanding one of all is the cathedral. Its iron steeple weighs 9,000 tonnes and was completed in 1882. It is the tallest one in France and it dominates Rouen, of which it is the symbol, from the top of its 152 metres (494 ft.). Supported by the St. Romain's Tower and Butter Tower, lit by its rose window, the west front has been described as a "cliff of carved stone". Its doorways are a poor man's Bible, written with a stonemason's chisel. The nave, transept, chancel, and crypt are equally rich in architectural terms. Around the chancel and in the Lady Chapel are the tombs of a number of illustrious figures who wrote the history of Normandy.

Since the 4th Century, each period has added something to the cathedral; ours almost destroyed it. It was hit by seven torpedoes in 1944 and was only saved thanks to the daring and genius of a local builder, Georges Lanfry. It took twelve years' work to make the cathedral safe for use again by worshippers and only a never-ending round of maintenance work ensures that it remains the "most outstanding building in Upper Normandy".

Just a few steps away in the delightful old town of Rouen, within the sound of the peal of bells

The spire seen from the Calende Door.

120

Centre Guillaume le Conquérant

Rue de Nesmond
F. 14400 BAYEUX
Tél. (33) 02.31.51.25.50

Nous vous remercions de votre visite et nous restons à votre disposition pour vous faire parvenir par courrier, toutes brochures, reproductions éditions, cartes postales, etc..

Demandez notre catalogue à l'adresse ci-dessus, nous vous fournirons tous les renseignements et conditions d'envois par retour.

Thank you for your visit and we remain at your service to send by post all the brochures, reproductions, publications and postcards, etc..

Ask at the above address for our catalogue. We will send you all the details and conditions for postage by return.

Bedankt sich fuer Ihren Besuch und bleibt durch ihren verfaufsdienst zu Ihrer Verfuegung um Ihren saemtliche Prospekte, Reproduktionen, Auflagen, Postkarten, usw. zukommen zu lassen.

Verlangen Sie bitte bei der oben angegebenen Adresse unseren Katalog. Wir Schicken Ihnen gerne postwendend alle Auskuenfte und Versandbedingungen.

A adresser à :
To send to :
Bestellung senden an :

TAPISSERIE DE BAYEUX
Centre Guillaume le Conquérant
Rue de Nesmond
F. 14400 BAYEUX

Je désire recevoir votre catalogue de reproductions

Nom – Name :

Adresse – Adress – Adresse :

Pays – Country – Land :

"As soon as one sets foot in the cathedral,... one feels a sense of awe..."
(Stendhal, Memories of a Tourist).

on Notre-Dame, is the Church of St. Ouen. This is a minster, with, as its entrance, the famous Urchins' Door (*portail des Marmousets*). The nave is 137 metres (445 ft.) long. Nowhere else has Gothic architecture achieved such purity and such ethereal beauty, while at the same time letting so much light in beneath its vaulted roof. The impression of peace and containment is even easier to appreciate because of the very austere interior decoration which leaves plenty of time to admire the architecture and the splendid 14th and 16th-century stained-glass windows that illuminate the chancel and nave.

At the end of the dark Rue Saint-Romain is St. Maclou's Church built between 1437 and 1517. This is the Flamboyant Gothic style in all its glory. Its porch has five arches projecting beyond the west front. The exuberance and finesse of the carvings in the porch and on the doorways is an indication of the degree of perfection reached by the stone masons and stonecutters in Rouen at that time.

The graveyard at St. Maclou's Church is part of the religious tour. Set up in the 16th Century after the plague epidemic, it is an amazing cemetery. Pillars and beams form the framework of the buildings and all have been carved with skulls, gravediggers' tools and other funereal emblems while, on a fresco that has unfortunately been damaged, Death is shown leading princes and prelates in a dance.

The Gothic and Classical chapel built by the Jesuits who founded the college (now the Corneille High

A tour of Normandy

School), the churches of St. Godard and St. Patrick (the latter has some of the finest stained-glass windows in France), and the Church of St. Nicaise which is a delightful combination of 13th-century and modern architecture are some of the other churches worth a visit in Rouen. St. Romain's, which has recently been restored, is a fine example of 18th-century architecture and it houses the red marble tomb of the Bishop of Rouen who, c. 700 A.D, became its patron saint after delivering it from the monster that was terrorising the town, the Gargoyle.

The modern Church of St. Joan of Arc on Place du Vieux-Marché is lit up by the stained-glass windows from St. Vincent's Church which was destroyed during the war. It tugs the heart strings as well as touching a chord for its aesthetic beauty for it marks the spot on which the young shepherdess from Domrémy reached the end of her life. The tour runs from 102 Rue Jeanne-d'Arc where she was imprisoned in Bouvreuil Castle and leads to

Timbered housefronts: one of the charms of Rouen.

the "Joan of Arc Tower" where she was threatened with torture, then to the gardens round St. Ouen's Church where she abjured her faith and to Rue Saint-Romain where, in the Officialité, she was rehabilitated in 1456. It ends at Place du Vieux-Marché where, on 30th May 1431, she was burnt at the stake as a witch. "The tomb of heroes is the heart of the living", says a quotation from Malraux.

Literature is another theme for a tour. Of all the writers born in Rouen, Pierre Corneille and Gustave Flaubert are the best-known. The house where the poet and dramatist lived, now a museum, stands on Rue de la Pie, a tall narrow frontage of stone and timber. As to the novelist, he was born in the hospital in which his father was the senior consultant. The apartment that he lived in is now a museum but it shares its rooms with the Museum of Medicine. Other names worthy of a mention include Saint-Amant, Madame Le Prince de Beaumont, Pradon, Fontenelle, Maurice Leblanc, Salacrou etc. As to Maupassant, Gide, Alain, Maurois, Bernanos and Mac Orlan, they spent longer or shorter periods of their life in Rouen and it has been mentioned in their works. Those who simply passed through, but again wrote about the town, are too numerous to mention. They range from Madame de Sévigné to

The church dedicated to Joan of Arc.

The Finance Office, now the Tourist Office.

Saint-Simon, from Stendhal, Michelet, Hugo, Nodier, and Balzac to Zola and, of course, Jean de La Varende.

As the fifth largest port in France, the world's leading port for wheat exports and the third largest river port, Rouen is the gateway to the ocean for Paris. The Seine has therefore provided the city with its wealth from the days of the Dukes of Normandy onwards and even more so during the Renaissance. Even if it has moved away from the centre compared to its location of old, the harbour, which has connections as far away as Honfleur, remains the heart of the town.

Rue du Gros-Horloge was the first pedestrian precinct in France. It is also the busiest street in Rouen and one from which the ornateness of the vernacular architecture can be seen at its best. These buildings sometimes tend to be forgotten because of the religious architecture. The Great Clock, which stands at the foot of the belfry, is the most popular sight in Rouen.

Gustave Flaubert, honoured in Rouen and Ry.

The law courts, just a few yards from Rue du Gros-Horloge, is the local people's pride and joy. Enter the main courtyard from Rue des Juifs (archaeological digs have recently revealed the existence of a synagogue on the site, destroyed in the 12th Century) if you want to appreciate the full beauty of its façades, richly decorated with pinnacles and bellcotes, and its huge main staircase.

During hearings visitors can enter the Assizes, the courtroom with a coffered ceiling "of terrifying beauty" that so impressed Michelet the historian. The lobby, once the Prosecutors' Chamber, has a wonderful wood-panelled roof. The dramatist Corneille could be heard filing pleas here when he was still a barrister.

Vernacular architecture in Rouen also includes the Bourgtheroulde Residence on which the façade is decorated with two magnificent friezes. There is also the Exchequer opposite the cathedral, the majestic buildings that house the Town Hall (all that remain of the

Rue du Gros-Horloge.

abbey buildings of St. Ouen's), numerous fountains like the huge St. Mary Fountain, some breath-taking private mansions such as the ones on Place Rougemare, and the no less numerous half-timbered houses. Many of them were demolished from 1850 onwards or their frontage was given a coating of plasterwork. Large numbers of them have, though, been restored over the past few decades and have given Rouen town centre back all the charm that it had before the demolitions of the 19th Century.

The museums are as impressive as the city's history. The Art Gallery is one of the most prestigious in France with almost 3,000 paintings, 7,000 drawings, and 400 pieces of sculpture. Géricault, who was born in Rouen, is well-represented but there are few great masters whose work does not hang here.

The La Secq des Tournelles Museum contains more than 12,000 items of utilitarian or decorative wrought-ironwork dating from the 12th to the 19th Centuries. In the old Hocqueville Residence, the Ceramics Museum displays in all their splendour pieces of "Old Rouen" famous for the quality of the pinks and blues.

The *département's* Antiquities Museum contains a number of masterpieces from the abbeys, churches, or mere private homes destroyed during the French Revolution or during the renovation work in Rouen in the 19th Century. The Natural History Museum may have supplied Flaubert with the idea for the parrot in *Un coeur simple*. The Education Museum is housed in one of the superb half-timbered residences known as the Four Aymon Sons' House.

A visit to Rouen, though, is never finished. So before you set off again, perhaps you might find time to read the lines written by the old troubadour Robert Wace who imagines Rollo looking at the town whose fortune he was about to make by designating it capital of Normandy:

Et dedans et dehors séduit la regarda
Elle lui sembla plaisante et belle
Avec force lui plut et le charma icelle.
(He looked at her within and without
She seemed to him pleasant and beautiful
Pleased him greatly and delighted him.)

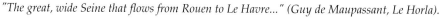

"The great, wide Seine that flows from Rouen to Le Havre..." (Guy de Maupassant, Le Horla).

"When all Hope is born again" (Frédéric Bérat, Ma Normandie).

A tour of Normandy

MANCHE

AURIGNY

GUERNESEY

SERCQ

JERSEY

Cherbourg

Barfleur

Diélette

Valognes

Saint-Vaast-la-Hougue

Bricquebec

Sainte-Mère-Église

PLAGES DU DÉBARQUEMEN

UTAH

OMAHA

CÔTE DE NACRE

GOLD

JUNO

COTENTIN

Carteret

Saint-Sauveur-le-Vicomte

Isigny

Arromanches

Courseulles

SWORD

Cab

Bayeux

Ouistreham

PARC NATUREL RÉGIONAL
DES MARAIS DU COTENTIN
ET DU BESSIN

Lessay

CAEN

Tilly-sur-Seulles

CALVADO

SAINT-LÔ

BESSIN

Coutances

Aunay-sur-Odon

N158

MANCHE

BOCAGE
NORMAND

Clécy

Falais

Villedieu-les-Poêles

SUISSE NORMANDE

Granville

Vire

Condé-sur-Noireau

BAIE DU
MONT-SAINT-MICHEL

La-Haye-Pesnel

BASSE-NORMANDIE

Orne

Flers

Saint-Malo

MONT-SAINT-MICHEL

Avranches

Mortain

PASSAIS

ORNE

Dinard

Saint-Hilaire-du-Harcouet

Domfront

Bagnoles-de-l'Orne

Carro

SAINT-BRIEUC

N176 - E401

Séline

PARC NATUREL RÉGIC
NORMANDIE-MAIN

Dinan

E401

Combourg

A84

N12 - E50

Rance

N137

Fougères

Couesnon

N12

Mayenne

BRETAGNE

N164

N12

PAYS DE LA LOIR

Montfort

RENNES

Vilaine

A81 - E50

LAVAL

0 10 20 30 40 50 km

A tour of Normandy

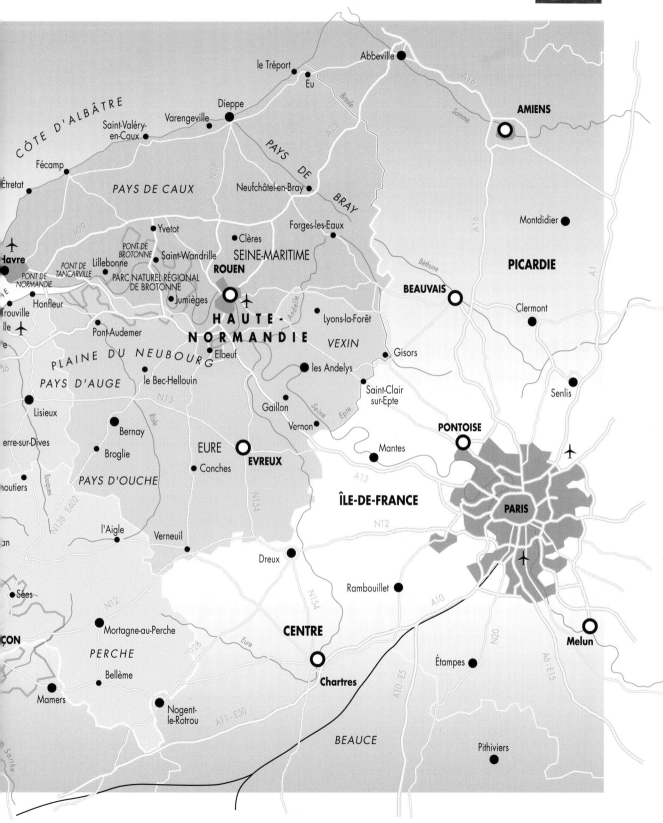

127

Table of contents

Front cover:
The cliffs and "Needle Rock" in Etretat (Seine-Maritime)
Backcover:
Coupesarte, a manor house in the Auge region (Calvados)

Cartography: *Philippe Rekacewicz*

Impression et reliure : Pollina s.a., 85400 Luçon - n° 73623-C
I.S.B.N. 2.7373.1718.5 - Dépôt légal : avril 1996
N° d'éditeur : 3139.02.06.01.98